2023 EDITION
POOL MAINTENANCE LOGBOOK INCLUDED

THE COMPLETE POOL MAINTENANCE HANDBOOK

THE POOL CARE BIBLE - A STEP-BY-STEP GUIDE TO CRYSTAL CLEAR WATER AND POOL CHEMISTRY ALL YEAR ROUND, SAVING TIME & MONEY,

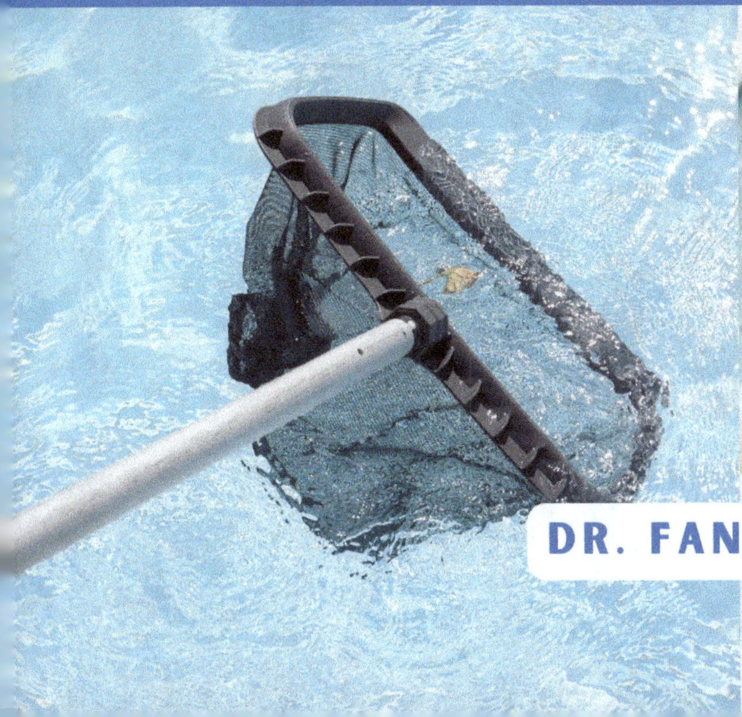

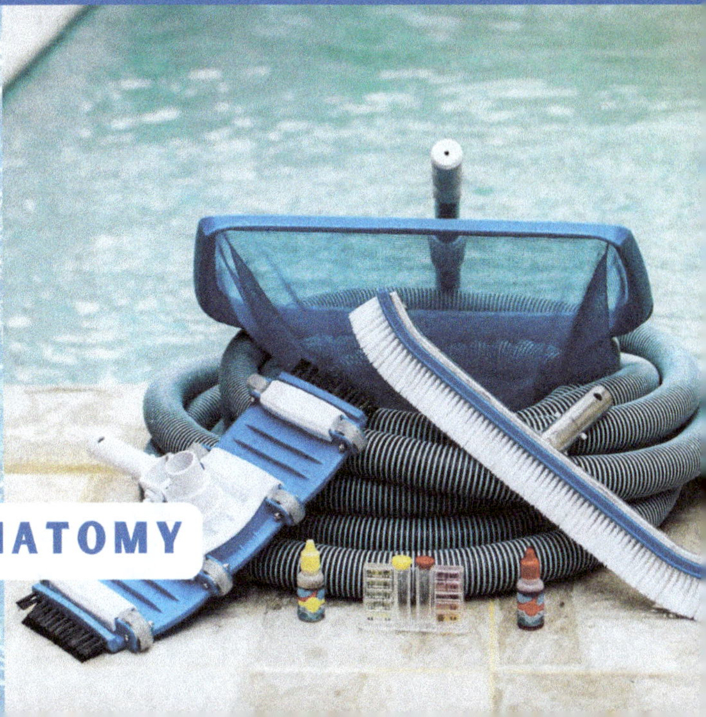

DR. FANATOMY

copyright@ dr. fanatomy 2023

All rights reserved. No part of this publication may be reproduced, distributed, or transmitted in any form or by any means, including photocopying, recording, or other electronic or mechanical methods, without the prior written permission of the publisher, except in the case of brief quotations embodied in critical reviews and certain other noncommercial uses permitted by copyright law.

This book is a work of non-fiction , and any resemblance to actual persons, living or dead, or actual events is purely coincidental.

The information and techniques described in this book are intended for educational and informational purposes only. The author and publisher shall not be held liable for any injury, damage, or loss arising from the use or misuse of the information presented in this book.

While every effort has been made to ensure the accuracy of the information contained within this book, the author and publisher make no warranties or representations, express or implied, about the completeness, accuracy, reliability, suitability, or availability with respect to the contents of this book for any purpose. The use of any information provided in this book is at the reader's own risk.

TABLE OF CONTENTS

1. INTRODUCTION TO POOL MAINTENANCE: UNDERSTANDING THE BASICS
(Pg: 7-14)

Section 1: The Wonderful World of Pools

- What makes pools so appealing?
- How can owning a pool enhance your lifestyle?
- Exploring the different types of pools and their characteristics.
- Is pool ownership right for you?

Section 2: Explore Pool Components

- What are the essential components of a pool?
- 5 essential components of a pool with maintenance tips
- Understanding the roles of the pump, filter, skimmer, and other key parts.
- How do these components work together to keep your pool clean and functional?

2. TYPES OF POOLS: CHOOSING THE PERFECT OASIS
(Pg: 15-25)

Section 1: In-Ground Pools

- What are in-ground pools, and what are their advantages and considerations?
- Exploring different in-ground pool designs and materials.
- How to maintain and care for an in-ground pool.

Section 2: Above-Ground Pools

- What are above-ground pools, and what are their benefits and considerations?
- Limitations of above-ground pool
- Exploring different above-ground pool options and features.
- How to maintain and care for an above-ground pool.

3. ESSENTIAL POOL MAINTENANCE TOOLS AND EQUIPMENT
(Pg: 26-36)

Section 1: Must-Have Pool Maintenance Tools

- What is pool maintenance?
- Importance of regular pool maintenance.
- Health and safety considerations.
- What tools do you need to keep your pool clean and well-maintained?
- Choosing the right tools for your pool's specific needs

Section 2: Pool Equipment and Accessories

- Exploring various pool equipment, such as pumps, filters, heaters, and timers.
- Understanding the importance of proper installation and maintenance of pool equipment.
- What additional accessories, which are useful?

4. WATER CHEMISTRY: ACHIEVING AND MAINTAINING BALANCE
(Pg: 37-45)

Section 1: The Fundamentals of Water Chemistry

- Why is water chemistry crucial for pool maintenance?
- Understanding pH, chlorine, alkalinity, and other key chemical parameters.
- How to test and adjust water chemistry effectively.

Section 2: Preventing and Treating Algae and Green Water

- Why do algae grow in pools, and how can it be prevented?
- Exploring different types of algae and their treatment methods.
- How to maintain clear and algae-free water.

5. SKIMMING, BRUSHING, AND VACUUMING: KEEPING YOUR POOL CLEAN
(Pg: 46-55)

Section 1: Skimming: Removing Surface Debris

- How to use a skimmer net to remove leaves, bugs, and other debris from the pool's surface.
- Why is regular skimming important for pool maintenance?

Section 2: Brushing: Eliminating Dirt and Algae

- How to properly brush the pool walls, steps, and floor to prevent dirt and algae buildup.
- Which type of brush should you use for different pool surfaces?

Section 3: Vacuuming: Deep Cleaning Your Pool

- Understanding the different types of pool vacuums and their usage.
- Step-by-step instructions for effectively vacuuming your pool to remove debris and dirt.

6. CIRCULATION AND FILTRATION: KEEPING THE WATER CLEAR
(Pg: 56-63)

Section 1: The Importance of Proper Circulation

- Why is water circulation essential for pool maintenance?
- Understanding the role of the pump and the circulation system.
- How to optimize water flow and distribution in your pool.

Section 2: Exploring Pool Filtration Systems

- Understanding different types of filters (sand, cartridge, and DE) and their pros and cons.
- How to clean and maintain your pool filter for optimal performance.

7. POOL SAFETY AND ESSENTIAL GUIDELINES
(Pg: 64-70)

Section 1: Creating a Safe Pool Environment

- What are the most important tools for pool safety?
- What are the functionalities of various safety tools?

Section 2: Guidelines for Safe Pool Use

- What are the tips for a safe pool season?
- What are the best practices for pool property with kids and pets?

8. TROUBLESHOOTING COMMON POOL ISSUES
(Pg: 71-84)

Section 1: Dealing with Water Imbalance

- Understanding the causes and effects of imbalanced water chemistry.
- Preventing scale buildup and staining.

Section 2: Managing Algae and Green Water

- Table: Algae types, their causes, and how to get rid of them
- Managing Algae

Section 3: Addressing Equipment Problems

- Common pump issue with resolution
- Common filter issue with resolution
- Common heater issue with resolution
- Table: Common Equipment - problems, causes, solution

9. OFF-SEASON MAINTENANCE AND WINTERIZING

(Pg: 85-93)

Section 1: Preparing for the Off-Season

- Why is off-season maintenance important?
- Tips on winterizing your pool
- Tips for reopening and preparing the pool for the next swimming season
- Steps/Workflow - Winterize and Reopening

Section 2: Winterizing Your Pool

- How to protect your pool from freezing temperatures and winter weather conditions.
- Draining, covering, and maintaining the pool during the off-season.
- Tips for reopening and preparing the pool for the next swimming season.

10. GLOSSARY & FREQUENTLY ASKED QUESTIONS (FAQS)

(Pg: 94-102)

Section 1: Glossary

Section 2: Frequently Asked Questions (FAQs)

11. POOL MAINTENANCE LOGBOOK

(Pg: 103-112)

Table 1: Pool Water Chemistry Log

Table 2: Pool Maintenance Schedule

Table 3: Pool Water Test Results

Table 4: Pool Chemical Inventory

Table 5: Pool Equipment Maintenance Log

Table 6: Pool Cleaning Log

Table 7: Pool Maintenance Expenses

Table 8: Pool Safety Checklist

Table 9: Pool Water Temperature Log

Table 10: Pool Cover Usage Log

CONCLUSION

"Pool maintenance is like dancing with nature, finding balance in the rhythm of water and chemistry."

1. Introduction to Pool Maintenance: Understanding the Basics

Section 1: The Wonderful World of Pools

Welcome to the Wonderful World of Pools! This section will explore why pools are so exciting and how having a pool can upgrade your lifestyle.

What makes pools so appealing?

- Swimming is a "Fun" workout. It helps in weight loss, improves strength & stamina, boosts overall body flexibility, and is great for heart health.

- Nowadays, when everyone is stressed, swimming is a great tool to fight mental and physical stress.

- While everyone is buried in their mobiles, laptops, and other digital gadgets, It's a great way to socialize and spend quality time with your loved ones.

- It helps in injury recovery and is one of the best things to do before you hit bed if you are struggling to sleep.

Family having fun together

How can owning a pool upgrade your life your lifestyle?

Owning the pool is a great feeling! It contributes to good health, mood, and quality family time in your everyday life.

Regular swimming can improve the cardiovascular system, develop strong muscles, and boost immunity. Swimming also helps us relax by reducing stress and improving overall wellness.

In addition, a pool can be a place for gathering, partying, hosting celebrations, and events that unite people.

What are the different types of pools?

There are multiple options for swimming pools based on cost, area, shape, size, and type of residence (temporary or permanent).

In-Ground swimming pools are a popular option for a permanent structure in your backyard. They can be personalized to match your choices and blend seamlessly with your home and outdoor landscape.

Above-Ground pools supply an even more cost-effective and portable option, making them popular for those with limited area, budget, and moving frequently. Knowing about various types of swimming pools will assist you in making an informed choice that matches your requirements and situation.

In-Ground   Above-Ground

Is pool ownership right for you?

Swimming pool ownership comes with responsibility and financial implications. Before you take the plunge, please look over whether you have the time, finances, and patience to own a swimming pool.

Factors such as the climate in your region, availability of local resources, and specialist services in case of emergency ought to be carefully planned. Also, insurance and local municipality rules must be considered before deciding on a pool.

In this book, we will assist you with the basics of swimming pool maintenance, ensuring **you have the expertise and self-confidence to make an informed decision.**

Section 2: Explore Pool Components

Welcome to the world behind the beautiful pool! In this section, we will dive into the essential components of a swimming pool and how they work together to keep your swimming working with crystal-clean blue water!

What are the essential components of a pool?

A swimming pool has multiple components that work together to keep it clean and functional. Each component is crucial in your pool water's flow, filtration, and sanitization. When all these components work in sync, you enjoy those dives. Any issue arises when they break down or do not function properly.

Below are the most important components of pool anatomy:

- **Pump:** A pump is called the heart of the pool as It filters the water and circulates it back into the pool. The pump's size depends on the pool's size.

- **Filter:** Filters keep pools clean by removing dirt and debris. Sand, cartridge, and D.E. filters are the three main types. A pool service provider can help you choose the right one for your needs.

- **Skimmer:** To keep the pool water clean and safe, the circulation process begins with the skimmers installed in the pool wall near the waterline. These skimmers have a basket that captures floating debris, such as leaves and insects. They can also serve as a means to distribute chlorine throughout the pool.

- **Main Drains:** The function of the main drain in a swimming pool is similar to that of a skimmer. It is situated in the deep end at the pool's bottom and serves as a suction outlet to improve water circulation. In in-ground pools, there are usually two main drains.

- **Return Lines:** The return lines transport the water to the pool once the water passes through the filter. These PVC piping lines terminate at the return jets.

- **Return Jets:** Inground pools typically have 2 or 3 small holes on the walls known as return jets. These jets inject the pool with newly filtered water. On the other hand, above-ground pools only utilize one return jet.

- **Chemical Feeders:** Chemical feeders can supply your pool with chlorine, bromine, or minerals automatically, so you don't have to worry about placing tablets in the skimmer basket or using a floating dispenser.

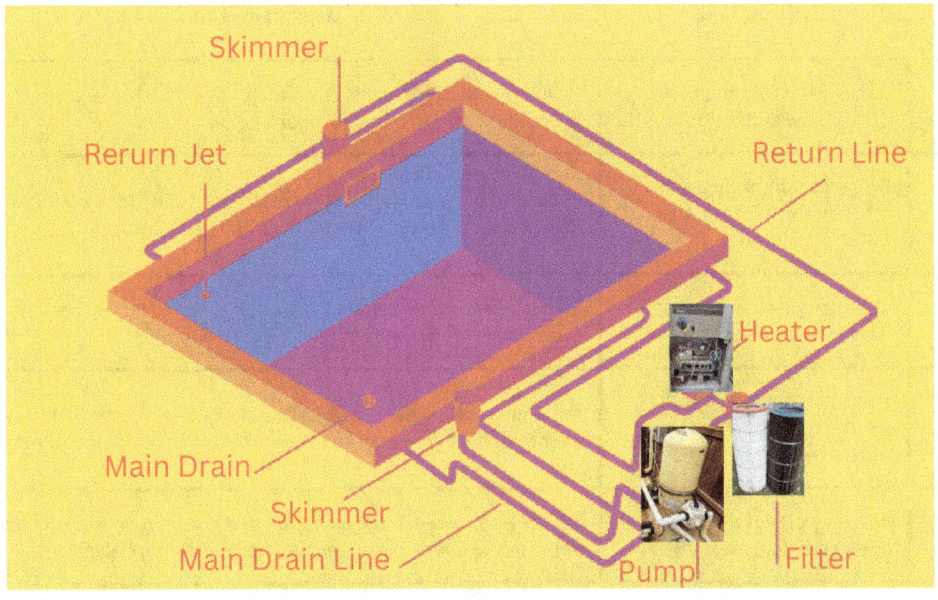

Pool Anatomy

CIRCULATION PROCESS

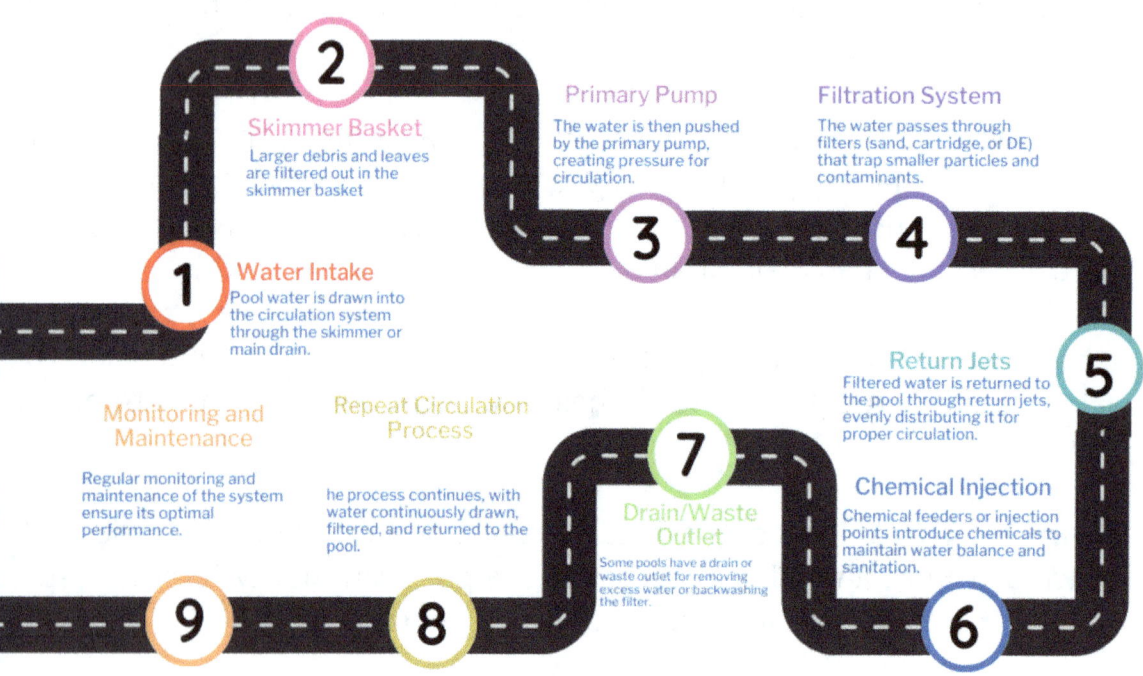

1. Water Intake — Pool water is drawn into the circulation system through the skimmer or main drain.

2. Skimmer Basket — Larger debris and leaves are filtered out in the skimmer basket.

3. Primary Pump — The water is then pushed by the primary pump, creating pressure for circulation.

4. Filtration System — The water passes through filters (sand, cartridge, or DE) that trap smaller particles and contaminants.

5. Return Jets — Filtered water is returned to the pool through return jets, evenly distributing it for proper circulation.

6. Chemical Injection — Chemical feeders or injection points introduce chemicals to maintain water balance and sanitation.

7. Drain/Waste Outlet — Some pools have a drain or waste outlet for removing excess water or backwashing the filter.

8. Repeat Circulation Process — The process continues, with water continuously drawn, filtered, and returned to the pool.

9. Monitoring and Maintenance — Regular monitoring and maintenance of the system ensure its optimal performance.

5 essential components of a pool with maintenance Tips

Component	Description	Maintenance Tips
Pump	Circulates water, maintaining proper flow and filtration.	Regularly check for leaks, clean the strainer basket, and ensure proper lubrication of moving parts.
Filter	Removes debris, dirt, and other impurities from the water.	Backwash or clean the filter regularly according to manufacturer's instructions. Replace filter media when necessary.
Skimmer	Collects debris and leaves from the water surface.	Empty the skimmer basket frequently, keeping it free from debris. Clean or replace the skimmer weir as needed.
Chlorinator	Dispenses chlorine or other sanitizing agents into the water.	Monitor chlorine levels regularly and adjust as needed. Clean and maintain the chlorinator to prevent clogging or malfunctioning.
Water Chemistry	Balances pH, alkalinity, and other chemical parameters.	Test the water regularly, adjust pH and alkalinity levels, and add appropriate chemicals to maintain proper water balance.

What are the roles of the pump, filter, skimmer, and other key parts?

The pump is the **heart of your pool's circulation system,** in charge of drawing water from the pool, passing it through the filter, and returning it to the pool. The filter traps debris, impurities, and pollutants, ensuring the water remains clean and clear.

The skimmer acts as a first line of defense, capturing fallen leaves, pests, and other debris floating on the pool's surface.

Other components, such as the return jets and pipe connections, facilitate the correct flow and distribution of water throughout the pool.

Skimmer Net

Pump

How do these components work together to keep your pool clean and functional?

Recognizing how these components work in unison is essential for keeping a healthy, balanced, and welcoming pool.

The **pump** distributes the water, ensuring it travels through the filter, where impurities are caught and removed.

The **skimmer** prevents particles from sinking to the bottom of the swimming pool, maintaining the water clean.

Finally, the **return jets** assist in distributing the filtered water back into the swimming pool, keeping the proper flow and avoiding stagnant water.

By understanding the roles and functions of each component, you'll be much better prepared to repair problems and do required pool maintenance tasks.

In this chapter, we have embarked on a journey into the basics of pool maintenance. We have explored the benefits, considerations, and types of swimming pools.

Additionally, we have looked into the essential components of a pool and how they work together to keep your swimming pool clean and useful.

Equipped with this knowledge, you are ready to dive deeper into swimming pool upkeep and unlock the tricks to maintaining a beautiful and welcoming swimming pool.

Below are photographs of a robotic skimmer I bought recently and a return jet fixed at the side wall of my pool. The skimmer helps in collecting surface debris automatically and return jet transfer filtered water back to the pool.

Robotic Skimmer

Return Jets

2. Types of Pools: Choosing the Perfect Oasis

Section 1: In-Ground Pools

This section will discuss in-ground pools in detail, reviewing their benefits, considerations, style options, and maintenance needs. The aim is that after this chapter, you should be clear about which pool meets your need.

What are in-ground pools, and what are their advantages and considerations?

In-ground swimming pools are a prominent choice among homeowners looking for a long-lasting, lavish pool service. These pools are created by excavating a hole in the ground and building a swimming pool framework.

There are several benefits to having an in-ground swimming pool:

- **Layout Flexibility**: Regarding in-ground swimming pools, many layout options are available to help you create a visually appealing pool that complements your outdoor space.

- **Size and Depth Options**: In-ground pools supply higher adaptability regarding size and depth, enabling you to personalize the pool to accommodate your details, requirements, and preferences.

- **Property Worth:** A properly designed and correctly preserved in-ground pool can dramatically improve your property value, making it an attractive financial investment for homeowners.

In-Ground Pool

Nonetheless, there are a couple of factors to consider to keep in mind:

Price: Regarding upfront costs, in-ground ones require a higher initial investment than above-ground options. This is due to various expenses like excavation, construction, materials, and additional features such as decking and landscaping.

Installation/Construction Time: Structuring an in-ground swimming pool requires more time and preparation than setting up an above-ground swimming pool. The building and construction process can take several weeks and even months, depending on the complexity of the style.

Specialist Aid: If you're looking to install an in-ground pool, working with skilled professionals with the expertise and necessary equipment for a proper and safe setup is important. Choosing a reputable swimming pool service provider can ensure a successful installation.

Exploring different in-ground pool designs and materials

When it involves in-ground swimming pools, there are various design choices and products to select from:

Standard Rectangle-shaped Pools: Timeless and ageless, rectangle-shaped pools provide a smooth and elegant look. They are appropriate for lap swimming and are preferred for those who favor a more formal and symmetrical design.

Rectangular In-Ground Pool

Freeform Pools: Freeform pools are made with natural and flowing shapes, imitating natural bodies of water. They use a more unwinded and give all-natural feel, blending harmoniously with the bordering landscape.

Freeform In-Ground Pool

Vinyl Liner Pool

Vinyl Liner Pools: These swimming pools include a vinyl fabric liner that provides a smooth and comfy surface. Vinyl fabric linings are available in many patterns and colors, allowing for personalization and easy maintenance.

Fiberglass Pools: Fiberglass pools are pre-formed shells installed in the dug-deep location. They provide a quick installation process, low maintenance demands, and a smooth surface area that withstands algae growth.

Fiberglass Pool

Throughout the selection procedure, consider factors such as your personal preferences, the shapes and size of your backyard, and your spending plan.

I'd like to point out that consulting with swimming pool contractors or developers can help you figure out the most effective layout and product for your requirements.

How to maintain and care for an in-ground pool

Optimum maintenance is vital for keeping your in-ground swimming pool clean, secure, and pleasant.

Below are some crucial maintenance tasks for in-ground pools:

Water Chemistry: Consistently check the water and maintain appropriate chemical balance by adjusting pH, alkalinity, and sanitizer levels. This aids in preventing algae growth, bacteria accumulation, and other water impurities.

Maintenance of the Filtering System: The pool's filter should be cleaned regularly to remove debris and ensure optimal filtration. Then, per the manufacturer's advice, we must replace filter media or cartridges.

Skimming and Cleaning: To keep your pool clean, it's important to use a skimmer net to remove leaves, bugs, and any other debris from its surface. Once you've finished skimming, regularly vacuum the pool to eliminate any dust or debris that may have settled in it.

Brushing and Scrubbing: Brush the swimming pool wall surfaces and floor to avoid algae growth. Pay particular focus to corners, steps, and other hard-to-reach locations.

Pool Equipment Inspection: Consistently evaluate and preserve swimming pool equipment such as pumps, electric motors, and valves. Ensure they are operating appropriately and deal with any concerns immediately.

Winterization: If you stay in an area with cold winter times, effectively winterize your in-ground swimming pool to secure it from freezing temperatures. This includes reducing the water level, draining pipes, saving equipment, and adding wintertime chemicals.

By following a routine upkeep regimen and addressing any problems quickly, you can maintain your in-ground swimming pool in excellent condition and appreciate crystal-clear water throughout the swimming season.

Pool Maintenance

Section 2: Above-Ground Pools

This section will discover above-ground swimming pools, reviewing their advantages, considerations, options, and maintenance requirements.

What are above-ground pools, and what are their benefits and considerations?

Above-ground pools are popular for house owners searching for a budget-friendly, functional, and relatively easy-to-install swimming pool choice. Unlike in-ground pools, above-ground pools are created above the ground and typically feature a metal or resin framework with a vinyl lining. As a result, they offer several advantages:

Consider these points before deciding in-ground or above-ground pool:

- **One-time cost**: Above-ground swimming pools are generally much more budget-friendly than in-ground swimming pools, making them a pragmatic alternative for budget-conscious individuals or someone on the move.

- **Size and Depth Options**: In-ground pools provide customized size and depth options, enabling you to personalize the pool to accommodate your details, requirements, and preferences. Whereas the above-ground pool comes in a fixed shape and size as offered by the manufacturer.

- **Property Worth:** A properly designed and correctly preserved in-ground pool can dramatically improve your property value, making it an attractive financial investment for homeowners.

- **Portability**: Unlike in-ground swimming pools, above-ground swimming pools are portable and can be dismantled and transferred. This flexibility benefits those who move often or want to transform the swimming pool's area.

Easy Installation: Above-ground pools are reasonably quick and simpler to install than in-ground swimming pools. With proper prep work and the help of a few buddies or family members, you can have your pool up and running quickly.

Limitations of above-ground pool:

Regarding above-ground swimming pools, there are some limitations to keep in mind.

- Firstly, their **size and depth options** are typically more restricted than in-ground pools. Custom alternatives or an in-ground pool may be worth considering if you require a specific size or depth.

- In addition, while above-ground pools have improved in style choices, they still have some **design limitations** compared to in-ground pools. Their shape and appearance may be more standardized.

- It's also important to note that **safety** is crucial when it comes to above-ground swimming pools. Due to their elevated nature, safety precautions like secure fencing, ladders, and safe accessibility points are essential to prevent accidents, especially if you have children or pets.

Exploring different above-ground pool options and features

Above-ground pools are available in various sizes, forms, and attributes. Below are some alternatives you can explore:

- **Round Pools**: Round above-ground swimming pools are a standard option due to their simplicity and easy installation. They are offered in various sizes and can be an excellent option for smaller backyards.

- **Oval Swimming Pools:** Oval above-ground pools provide more space for swimming and are the right option for those who want a larger swimming pool. Their elongated form suits many yard designs.

Above-Ground Round Pool

Above-Ground Oval Pool

- **Semi-Inground Pools:** These pools are a hybrid of above-ground and in-ground styles, partially submerged for an attractive appearance and convenient entry.

Semi In-Ground Pool

During selection, consider your yard's area, budget, and preferred swimming pool shapes and size. In addition, product longevity and high quality are crucial.

How to maintain and care for an above-ground pool?

Proper maintenance is essential for keeping your above-ground pool clean, secure, and enjoyable. Below are some basic maintenance tasks:

- **Water Chemistry:** Consistently examine and balance the water chemistry, including pH, alkalinity, and sanitizer level. This helps preserve clear, healthy, balanced water and prevents algae development.

- **Filtering System Maintenance:** Clean or backwash the pool's filtration system according to the manufacturer's guidelines. Consistently check the filter cartridge or sand and also change them as needed. (Later, we will discuss types of filters.)

- **Surface Area Skimming and Cleansing:** Using a skimmer net removes fallen leaves, insects, and particles from the swimming pool's surface. Consistently vacuum or use a pool cleaner to remove dust and particles that have settled at the bottom surface.

- **Swimming Pool Wall and Lining Care**: Check the pool wall surfaces and lining for any indications of damage, wear, or tear. Repair any breaks or leaks promptly to stop further damage.

- **Winterization:** If you stay in an area with a harsh winter, effectively winterize your above-ground swimming pool to secure it from freezing temperatures. This involves reducing the water level, draining pipes, storing tools, and using winterizing chemicals.

If you want to enjoy refreshing swims all throughout the swimming season, it's important to follow a consistent maintenance routine and address any issues as soon as they arise.

This chapter covered a range of pool types, including in-ground and above-ground pools. We explored their respective benefits, factors to keep in mind when selecting a pool, design options, and upkeep requirements.

By understanding these factors, you'll be able to make an informed decision and select the pool that best meets your specific needs and preferences.

In the upcoming sections, we'll delve deeper into pool maintenance strategies and solutions for common problems, ensuring that you can fully enjoy your swimming pool.

Pool Cover -Winterization

3. Essential Pool Maintenance Tools and Equipment

Section 1: Pool Maintenance Tools

Pool Cleaning

What is Pool Maintenance?

Swimming pool care is keeping your pool clean, secure, and pleasant. It includes a variety of jobs, such as:

- Checking the water chemistry
- Vacuuming the pool
- Brushing the sides
- Skimming the surface
- Shocking the pool
- Cleaning up the filter
- Backwashing the pump
- Draining water through pipes as well as replenishing the swimming pool

The regularity of these tasks will certainly differ depending on the size and use of your pool.

However, an essential pool maintenance routine needs to consist of the following functions:

- **Daily**: Check the water chemistry and also change as required.
- **Weekly**: Vacuum the pool, brush the sides, and skim the surface area.
- **Monthly**: Clean the filter, and backwash the pump.
- **Quarterly**: Drain and fill up the pool.

Importance of Regular Pool Maintenance

A clean as well as properly maintained pool holds countless advantages for both the pool property owner as well as their guests.

By devoting time to routine swimming pool maintenance, you guarantee that your swimming pool remains enjoyable.

Below are some critical reasons that routine pool maintenance is necessary:

- **Improved aesthetics**: A well-maintained pool with clear water, balanced chemistry, and a clean surface improves the overall appearance of your backyard. It develops a pleasing environment and contributes to your property's overall look and feel.

Well Maintained Pool

- **Longevity of pool**: Regular maintenance assists in safeguarding your pool's structural integrity. It protects against algae, scaling, and rust and extends your pool's lifespan, saving you money on costly repair services.

- **Efficient working:** Right maintenance ensures your swimming pool runs at its best. It promotes efficient water flow, reliable purification, and balanced chemical levels, resulting in a swimming pool that is enjoyable to swim in and simple to preserve.

Health and Safety Considerations

Preserving a clean and appropriately sanitized pool is essential for the health and wellness of swimmers. Below's why:

- **Safety from waterborne disease:** Normal swimming pool maintenance, like keeping correct sanitizer levels and water balance, prevents the growth of hazardous bacteria, infections, and parasites that can trigger waterborne diseases. This saves the health of swimmers as well as minimizes the danger of infections.

Contaminated Pool

- **Algae and Contaminant Control**: By routinely skimming, brushing, as well as vacuuming your swimming pool, you stop algae development and also remove particles that can present pollutants. This guarantees that the water remains clean and clear, reducing the threat of skin and eye irritations.

What tools do you need to keep your pool clean and well-maintained?

When it comes to pool upkeep, having suitable devices is critical. So right here are the primary tools you'll require to keep your swimming pool clean and well-maintained :

- **Skimmer Net:** A skimmer net is used to remove fallen leaves, debris, and other floating objects from the surface of the swimming pool. It is essential to skim the water routinely to stop debris from sinking to the bottom. A net affixed to a long handle removes fallen leaves, debris, and pests from the water's surface area. Systematic skimming prevents debris from sinking to the bottom and also aids in maintaining water quality.

Skimmer Net

Pool Brush: A brush with stiff bristles to scrub the pool wall surfaces and floor to remove dust, algae, and other deposits. Cleaning protects against the buildup of algae as well as keeps the swimming pool surface areas clean.

Pool Brush

Pool Vacuum: There are numerous types of swimming pool vacuum cleaners, such as manual, automated, as well as robotic, which assist in removing dust as well as debris from the pool flooring and wall surfaces. Vacuuming ensures extensive cleaning as well as prevents the accumulation of particles that can impact water quality.

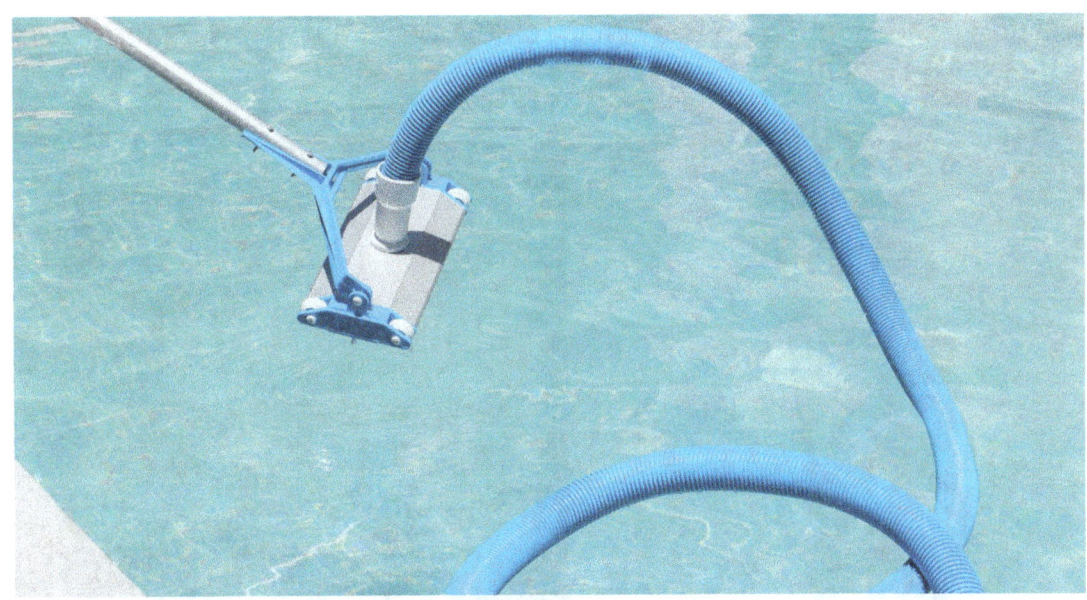

Pool Vacuum

Telescopic Pole: A telescopic pole is a functional tool that permits you to affix cleaning accessories such as nets, brushes, and vacuum heads. It can be extended till 12-16 feet, enabling you to get to all swimming pool areas.

Water Testing Kit: Examining the water routinely is critical for preserving well-balanced water chemistry. A water testing package will assist you in measuring and keeping an eye on specifications such as pH, chlorine levels, alkalinity, and calcium.

 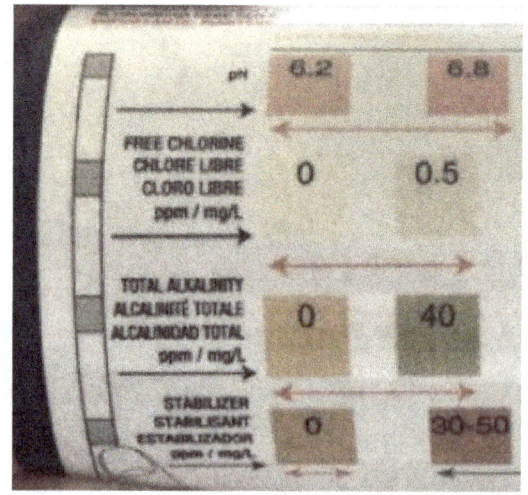

Water Testing Kit

Choosing the right tools for your pool's specific needs

When choosing swimming pool maintenance tools, consider the size and type of your swimming pool, the maintenance frequency, and your individual preferences.

Below are some ideas for picking the right devices for your swimming pool:

- Seek advice from a pool expert or seller to select tools appropriate for your pool type(plastic, concrete, fiberglass, and so on).

- Please consider the size of your pool and the type of debris which would be collected. Larger pools may need bigger or much more effective tools for efficient cleansing.

- Examine your pool care regularly and the time you can devote to maintenance. Robotic vacuums can be a practical alternative for those with limited time or physical restrictions.

- Pay attention to the customer reviews and use them to decide on the final purchase.

- Remember, having the right tools will simplify swimming pool maintenance and make it much more reliable, guaranteeing a clean and pleasurable swimming experience.

 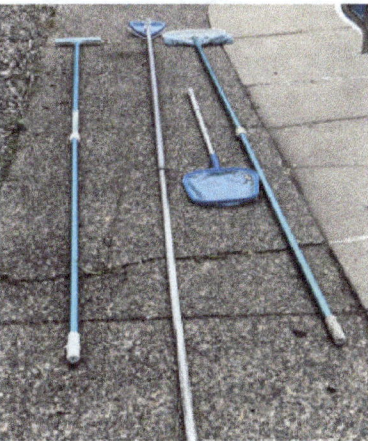

Water Cleaning tools

Section 2: Pool Equipment and Accessories

Exploring various pool equipment, such as pumps, filters, heaters, and timers?

Proper pool devices are essential for water circulation, filtering, heating, and automation. Right here are some critical pool devices components:

- **Swimming Pool Pump:** The swimming pool pump flows water through the filtration system, aiding in getting rid of debris and preserving water quality. It is the heart of your pool's circulation system.

- **Pool Filter**: The swimming pool filter removes impurities and debris from the water, keeping it tidy and clear. There are three significant filters: sand, cartridge, and diatomaceous earth (DE).

- **Pool Heating Unit**: Pool heating units enable you to regulate the water temperature level, providing convenience and prolonging your swimming season. Choices consist of gas, electric, and solar heaters.

Pool Pump

Pool Filter

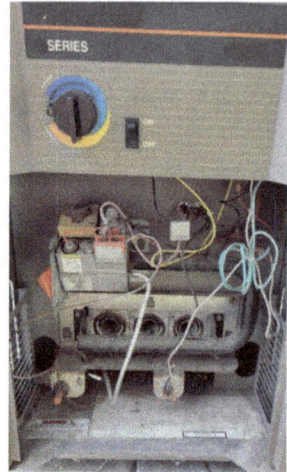
Heater

34

Pool Timer: A swimming pool timer automates the operation of your pool tools, enabling you to establish particular timetables for filtration, heating, and various other features. This helps maximize power efficiency as well as benefit.

Understanding the importance of proper installation and maintenance of pool equipment

Proper installation and maintenance of swimming pool devices are essential for their optimum efficiency and long life. Here are crucial considerations:

- For proper installation of links, electric requirements, and safety precautions, it is best to seek guidance from an expert or refer to the supplier guidelines.

- Frequently examine and clean up the devices to remove debris and lubricate components, as well as identify any indicators of wear or damage.

- Adhere to recommended maintenance routines for filter backwashing, pump basket cleaning, and cartridge or DE filter cleansing.

- Take note of water chemistry, as imbalances can affect tools performance. Maintain correct sanitizer levels and track calcium accumulation to stop damage.

What are other additional accessories which are useful?

Beyond the regular devices, various accessories can enhance your swimming pool experience. Consider the following options:

- **Pool Cover**: A pool cover avoids heating and thus reduces water evaporation. It also protects against debris from entering the pool when it's not being used.

- **Swimming Pool Steps or Ladders:** These provide simple and risk-free gain access in and out of the swimming pool, especially for above-ground swimming pools.

- **Pool Lights:** Mounting underwater or perimeter lights can develop an excellent ambiance for nighttime swimming.

- **Pool Security Tools**: Products such as pool alarm systems, security fences, and life-saving tools should be considered to ensure a secure pool setting.

- **Swimming Pool Maintenance Kits**: These kits typically include a combination of nets, brushes, vacuum cleaner heads, and other cleansing tools, offering a practical solution for routine maintenance.

Remember that the option of accessories depends upon your preferences and needs. However, they can enhance the safety, ease, and also overall health of your swimming pool.

Pool Lights

4. Water Chemistry: Achieving and Maintaining Balance

Section 1 : The Fundamentals of Water Chemistry

Welcome, pool lovers! In this chapter, we dive into the fascinating world of water chemistry. Comprehending the fundamentals of water chemistry is vital for achieving and maintaining a healthy, balanced, and welcoming swimming pool. So, let's get started!

Why is water chemistry crucial for pool maintenance?

Maintaining the right water chemistry is crucial for proper pool maintenance. It guarantees the water is safe, comfortable, and sparkling clear for you and your loved ones.

By maintaining the optimal chemical balance, we can prevent the growth of harmful microorganisms, control the occurrence of algae, and protect the longevity of your pool equipment.

Understanding pH, chlorine, alkalinity, and other key chemical parameters.

Let's acquaint ourselves with some essential chemical parameters that significantly affect the water quality of your swimming pool.

pH: Measuring the acidity or alkalinity of water is done through pH levels. A pH level of 7.0 is considered neutral, while maintaining pH levels between 7.2 and 7.8 is ideal for achieving maximum swimmer comfort and chemical effectiveness.

Chlorine: Chlorine is the most typical sanitizer used in swimming pools. It kills bacteria, viruses, and algae to keep the water secure and transparent. The recommended chlorine degree is generally between 1.0 and 3.0 parts per million (ppm).

weekly check maintenance test

Alkalinity: Alkalinity functions as a buffer to balance the pH to suitable levels. It is determined in parts per million (ppm) and must be kept between 80 and 120 ppm.

Calcium Hardness: Calcium hardness describes the degree of dissolved calcium in the water. Preserving appropriate calcium solidity (generally between 200 and 400 ppm) aids in stopping deterioration and also scaling issues.

How to test and adjust water chemistry effectively?

Regularly testing the water is essential for maintaining well-balanced water chemistry. You can use a water test kit to measure different parameters accurately. It's crucial to follow the instructions that come with the kit to obtain precise results.

If the results of the examination indicate that the chemical levels are outside of the recommended range, some adjustments may be necessary.

Below are some typical methods for changing water chemistry:

- **pH Adjustment**: Add soda ash or sodium bicarbonate to boost pH. To lower pH, muriatic acid or sodium bisulfate can be used.

- **Chlorine Adjustment**: Chlorine levels can be enhanced by adding chlorine tablets, liquid chlorine, or granular chlorine. If the chlorine degrees are too expensive, you can utilize a chlorine neutralizer or allow sunshine to deteriorate the chlorine naturally.

- **Alkalinity Adjustment**: Sodium bicarbonate (baking soda) is frequently used to increase alkalinity levels. To lower alkalinity, muriatic acid can be used.

Remember, it is necessary to make progressive modifications and retest the water after each adjustment to guarantee you achieve the desired balance.

pH Test

Section 2: Preventing & Treating Algae and Green Water

Why do algae grow in pools, and how can it be prevented?

Many pool owners face the issue of algae growth, which can quickly turn their clear water into a murky, green mess. To avoid this problem, it's essential to maintain and treat your pool routinely.

Algae can get in your pool from multiple sources, including wind, rainwater, and contaminated equipment or swimwear. Maintaining balanced water chemistry, sufficient water circulation, and regular sanitization is crucial to prevent algae from thriving.

Green Water due to Algae

Exploring different types of algae and their treatment methods

Algae are found in various forms, each requiring a different treatment strategy. One of the most common types includes green algae, yellow/mustard algae, and black algae. Let's discuss their attributes and also treatment methods:

Green Algae: This is the most common algae and typically transforms the water green. It can be treated by **shocking** the pool with a high chlorine dosage and using an algaecide especially developed to deal with green algae.

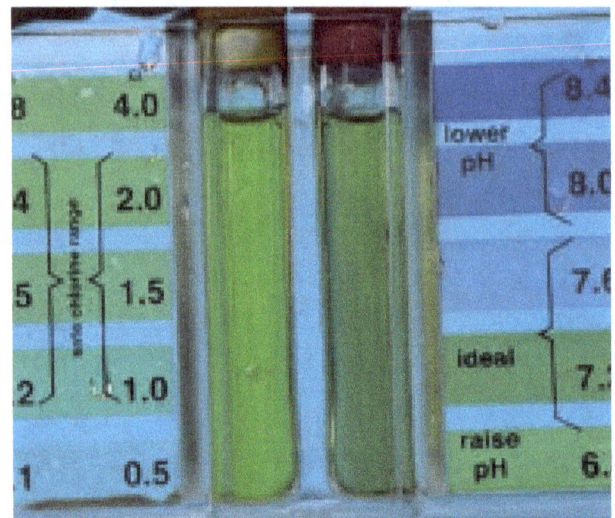
Test of green water

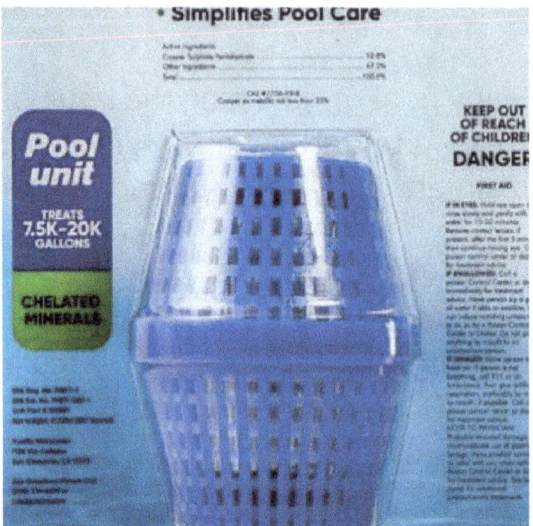
Algaecide

Algae Type	Causes	Remedy
Green Algae	Sunlight, warm temperatures, and poor pH balance	Shock treatment, algaecide, brushing
Yellow Algae	Poor water circulation and low sanitizer levels	Shock treatment, algaecide, brushing
Black Algae	Poor water circulation, low sanitizer levels, and rough pool surfaces	Brushing, algaecide, scrubbing with specialized tools

"**Shocking**" refers to introducing chlorine or non-chlorine pool chemicals into the water to elevate the level of "complimentary chlorine". The purpose is to increase this level to a point where impurities like algae, chloramines, and bacteria are eliminated.

Green Algae   Blue water after treatment

Yellow/Mustard Algae: If you spot yellow or mustard algae patches in your swimming pool, it's important to take an aggressive approach to get rid of them. This may involve brushing the affected areas, shocking the pool, and using specialized algaecides that are designed to be effective against these particularly resistant types of algae.

Mustard Algae

Black Algae: Black algae form stubborn, dark patches penetrating swimming pool surfaces. Treatment includes brushing with targeted chlorine application and using algaecides made for black algae.

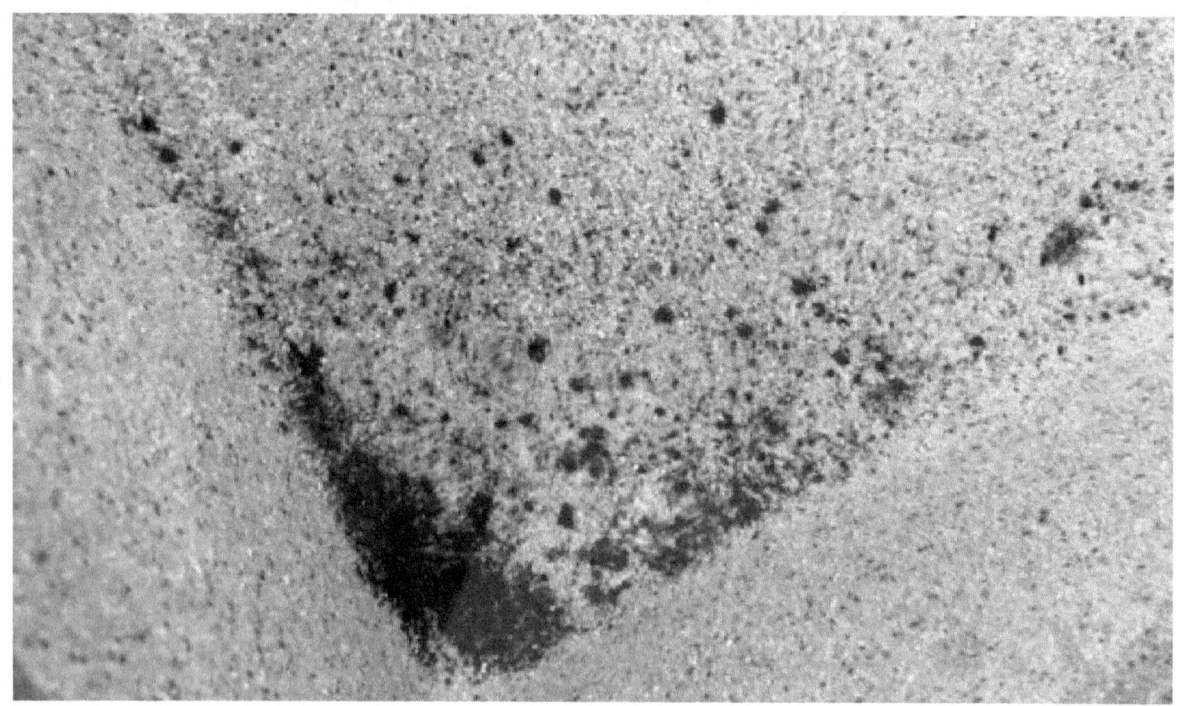

Black Algae

How to maintain clear and algae-free water.

Maintaining clear and algae-free water is crucial, and prevention is the key. Here are some tips to prevent the growth of algae:

- Regularly check and adjust water chemistry to ensure proper sanitizer levels.

- Run the swimming pool pump and filter for the recommended duration to maintain proper flow.

- Brush pool walls and surface areas frequently to prevent algae buildup.

- Cover the pool when not in use to reduce external contamination.

- Shock the swimming pool periodically to preserve high chlorine levels and kill any possible algae spores.

Well done! You've acquired valuable knowledge on water chemistry and preventing algae growth. Now, let's move on to the next chapter and explore effective pool cleaning techniques. Don't forget to grab your pool skimmer and let's keep this journey towards becoming pool maintenance experts going!

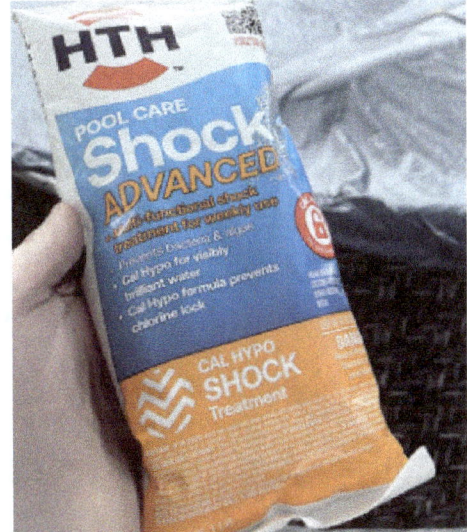

Shock Treatment

Brush

Pool Cover

5. Skimming, Brushing, and Vacuuming: Keeping Your Pool Clean

Section 1 : Skimming: Removing Surface Debris

Welcome back, swimming pool owners! In this chapter, we'll check out the essential tasks of skimming, brushing, and vacuuming to maintain a clean and inviting pool. Let's dive right in and start with the primary step: skimming.

How to use a skimmer net to remove leaves, bugs, and other debris from the pool's surface?

Maintaining a clean pool is crucial, and skimming is vital in removing unwanted particles that accumulate on the surface. Follow these simple steps to skim your swimming pool effectively:

- Ensure that your skimmer net is securely attached to the telescopic pole.

- Stand at the pool's edge and extend the pole to the farthest areas.

- Gently glide the skimmer net across the water's surface, collecting fallen leaves, bugs, and other debris.

- Once the net is full, remove it from the water and dispose of it in a designated debris bag or compost pile.

- Continue skimming until you have covered the entire pool surface, including edges and obstacles.

Skimmer Type	Main Function	Key Differences
Standard Skimmer	Removes floating debris from the pool surface.	Basic skimmer design, suitable for most pools.
Skimmer Basket	Collects debris before it enters the filtration system.	Includes a removable basket for easy cleaning.
Skimmer Sock	Traps finer particles and extends skimmer basket life.	Offers additional filtration and maintenance.
Automatic Skimmer	Automatically skims the pool surface for debris.	Programmable and reduces manual skimming efforts.

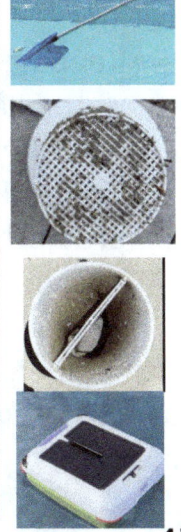

Skimmer Net

Why is regular skimming important for pool maintenance?

Regular skimming plays a critical part in keeping a clean as well as pleasant swimming pool environment. Here are a few reasons it is necessary:

- **Avoiding Clogged Filters**: Getting rid of debris from the surface area before it sinks to the bottom assists in avoiding blocking of pool filters, making specific optimal filtration efficiency.

- **Keeping Water Clean**: Skimming eliminates noticeable particles, boosting water clarity and improving the look of your swimming pool.

- **Controlling Algae Growth**: By eliminating leaves and other raw materials promptly, you minimize the nutrients available for algae development, assisting in maintaining your swimming pool algae-free.

Remember, constant skimming, particularly during peak debris periods, such as falls or windy season, is necessary to keep your swimming pool clear and inviting.

Section 2 : Brushing: Eliminating Dirt and Algae

Since we've done skimming, let's move on to the following step: brushing. Brushing the pool wall surfaces, steps, and flooring is necessary for protecting against dirt and algae buildup. Let's discover just how to do it efficiently.

How to properly brush the pool walls, steps, and floor?

- **Choose the Right Brush:** Select a pool brush that fits your pool's surface area product. Use a brush with stiff bristles for plaster or concrete swimming pools to avoid scratching; select a brush with softer bristles for plastic or fiberglass swimming pools.

- **Start at the Waterline:** Begin brushing at the waterline and gradually work down. Use long, sweeping motions to loosen dirt and algae from the walls. Pay additional interest to locations with visible discolorations or algae growth.

- **Brush the Steps and also Corners:** Don't fail to remember to brush the steps, corners, and other hard-to-reach locations where debris and algae tend to accumulate.

- **Brush the Pool Flooring**: As soon as you have finished brushing the walls and steps, carry on to the swimming pool floor. Once again, utilize long, sweeping activities to remove Dust or algae.

- **Repeat Consistently**: Aim to brush your pool at least as soon as a week to stop buildup and maintain a tidy, healthy, balanced environment.

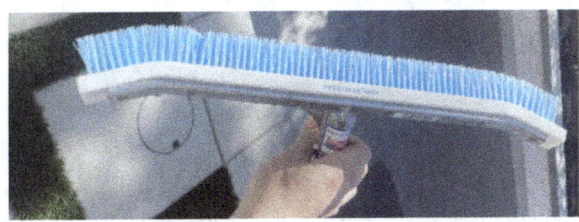
Brush for Concrete Pool Surface

Soft Brush for Plastic/Glass Pool Surface

Type of Pool Brush	Description	Usage
Nylon Bristle Brush	Soft nylon bristles that are gentle on pool surfaces.	Ideal for regular brushing of vinyl, fiberglass, or painted surfaces to remove debris and prevent algae buildup.
Stainless Steel Brush	Tough stainless steel bristles for heavy-duty cleaning.	Effective in removing stains, algae, and calcium buildup on concrete/plaster. Handle with care to avoid surface damage.
Wire Bristle Brush	Strong wire bristles designed for aggressive cleaning.	Used for heavy-duty cleaning on concrete or plaster surfaces with stubborn stains or algae growth. Requires caution to prevent surface damage.
Combo Bristle Brush	Combination of nylon and stainless steel bristles.	This brush can clean various pool surfaces with its nylon and stainless steel bristles.
Corner Brush	Specifically designed brush with a triangular shape.	Used for cleaning hard-to-reach corners, steps, and crevices in the pool where standard brushes may not reach effectively.

Which type of brush should you use for different pool surfaces?

Below are different pool surfaces and recommended brushes:

- **Plaster or Concrete Pool Surface**: Use a wire bristle or stainless steel bristles brush to eliminate dirt and algae from these surface areas.

- **Plastic or Fiberglass Pool Surface**: Choose a brush with softer nylon bristles to avoid scraping the pool's delicate surface area while properly removing debris.

Maintaining a clean and inviting swimming environment requires following certain methods and selecting the appropriate brush for your pool. With these measures in place, you can effectively keep dust and algae at bay.

Section 3 : Vacuuming: Deep Cleaning Your Pool

Now that we've skimmed and brushed our swimming pool, it's time for a deep clean using a vacuum cleaner.

Vacuuming removes particles and dust that may have settled on the swimming pool flooring. Check out the different kinds of swimming pool vacuums and learn how to use them successfully.

Below are various types of swimming pool vacuum cleaners and also their use.

There are three primary types of pool vacuum cleaners available.

Manual Vacuum Cleaner: This type of vacuum cleaner attaches to your pool's purification system and requires you to manually move the vacuum cleaner head throughout the swimming pool floor, utilizing the telescopic pole. It's a cost-effective choice but requires physical effort.

Manual Vacuum Cleaner

If your pool is large, expect to spend several hours cleaning it thoroughly. To make your hand vacuuming more comfortable, it's recommended to do some light hand cleaning before vacuuming.

When cleaning your swimming pool with a vacuum, it's important to be aware that the bristles may cause additional debris to be stirred up in the water. To ensure complete cleaning, it's recommended to backwash the pool's filter system after vacuuming, which may increase the amount of time required for the task.

Features :

- The mechanical option is more cost-effective and powerful compared to several automated systems.
- It requires hands-on work and patience to operate.
- The cleaning process may take several hours to ensure thoroughness.
- The swimming pool's filtration system needs frequent and regular backwashing to maintain optimal pressure.

Automatic Suction Vacuums

A vacuum for your pool that operates automatically through suction power is comparable to a whole-house vacuum cleaner system. To connect it to the water supply of the Filtration system, a hose is placed in the skimmer basket.

Once the pool's circulation pump is activated, the vacuum automatically navigates the vacuum head throughout the pool, picking up debris.

Suction-side pool cleaners require the pool pump to be active during the cleaning process, which consumes more electricity compared to other pool cleaners.

It is crucial to ensure that the filtration pump is in excellent working condition and powerful enough for the task. Additionally, you should expect to clean and backwash your filters regularly as they will collect more dirt than usual.

Features :

- Easy to maintain
- Cheaper than a robotic vacuum
- Durable option.
- The prerequisite is a pool with a running filtration system.
- It dumps everything into a pool filtration system.
- More energy requirements than manual system.

Automatic Vacuum Cleaner

Robotic Pool Vacuum

Self-contained robotic vacuum cleaners operate independently from your swimming pool's filtering system. They come equipped with their own filtering mechanism and power source.

Just position the robotic vacuum in the swimming pool to clean the pool flooring, walls, and steps. Robotic vacuum cleaners are highly effective and offer advanced attributes but are more expensive.

Features :

- Self-contained filtering system
- Most energy efficient
- Very easy to operate
- Expensive option

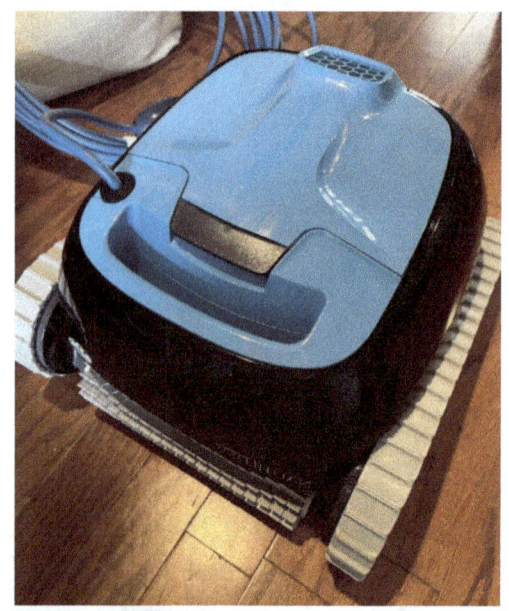

Robotic Vacuum Cleaner

In- Floor Pool Vacuum

Sophisticated in-ground pools often come equipped with in-floor automated vacuum systems integrated during the building process. Jets are strategically positioned at the bottom of the pool and linked to the filter system's return line.

When activated, the heads emerge, and a booster pump creates a high-pressure water current throughout the pool. This powerful wave sweeps along the pool's floor, directing dirt and debris toward the primary drains. The main pump extracts the particles from the pool as the water passes through the filtration system.

For those who can afford it, a pool service can also perform routine filter maintenance if they opt for an in-floor vacuum cleaner. This system adds significant value to the overall cost of pool construction.

Key features:

- Most expensive and can only be installed during pool construction
- Automated cleaning with minimal upkeep required.

In-Pool Vacuum Cleaner

6. Circulation and Filtration: Keeping the Water Clear

Section 1 : The Importance of Proper Circulation

Greetings, pool owners! Welcome to Chapter 6, where we'll discuss the crucial aspects of circulation and filtration systems necessary to keep your pool water clean and clear. Let's start by understanding the significance of proper circulation.

Why is water circulation vital for pool maintenance?

Water circulation plays a vital role in pool maintenance for several reasons:

Improved Water Quality: Proper circulation is essential in maintaining a clean and well-balanced swimming pool. It helps evenly distribute chemicals, preventing problems like growth in algae and cloudy water.

Particle Removal: Having a properly circulated swimming pool is essential for removing particles, dirt, and other contaminants. Water is redistributed through the circulation system, the skimmer, and the main drain, effectively gathering these unwanted substances and reducing the burden on the filtration system.

Temperature Control: Distributing the water helps distribute heat equally, preventing hot spots and preserving a comfortable swimming temperature.

Protecting Against Stagnant Water: Appropriate circulation prevents stagnant water, which can become a breeding ground for microorganisms, algae, and other contaminants. Flowing the water guarantees that all swimming pool locations receive appropriate filtering and chemical distribution.

Distributing Chemicals: Circulation helps evenly disperse pool chemicals, such as chlorine and pH balancers, throughout the pool. This ensures that the water continues to be effectively sterilized and stabilized, protecting against issues like algae development and water staining.

Enhancing Filtration Effectiveness: Efficient circulation guarantees that water travels through the filtration system regularly, using the filtering procedure best and capturing even more particles and impurities.

The main parts of your pool water circulation system are:

- Skimmers
- Main Drain
- Pump
- Filter
- Heater
- Chemical Feeder
- Returns.

Understanding the role of the pump and the circulation system.

The heart of your pool's circulation system is the pump, which is accountable for pushing water via the filtering system. Right here's precisely how the circulation process functions:

The circulation system comprises the pump, filter, pipes, and return jets. Below's just how it works:

- The pump pulls water through the skimmer(s) and primary drain pipe to keep the pool clean. It then pushes the water through the filtering system to remove impurities and particles.

- The filter efficiently captures fragments like dirt, leaves, and tiny organisms as the water flows through.

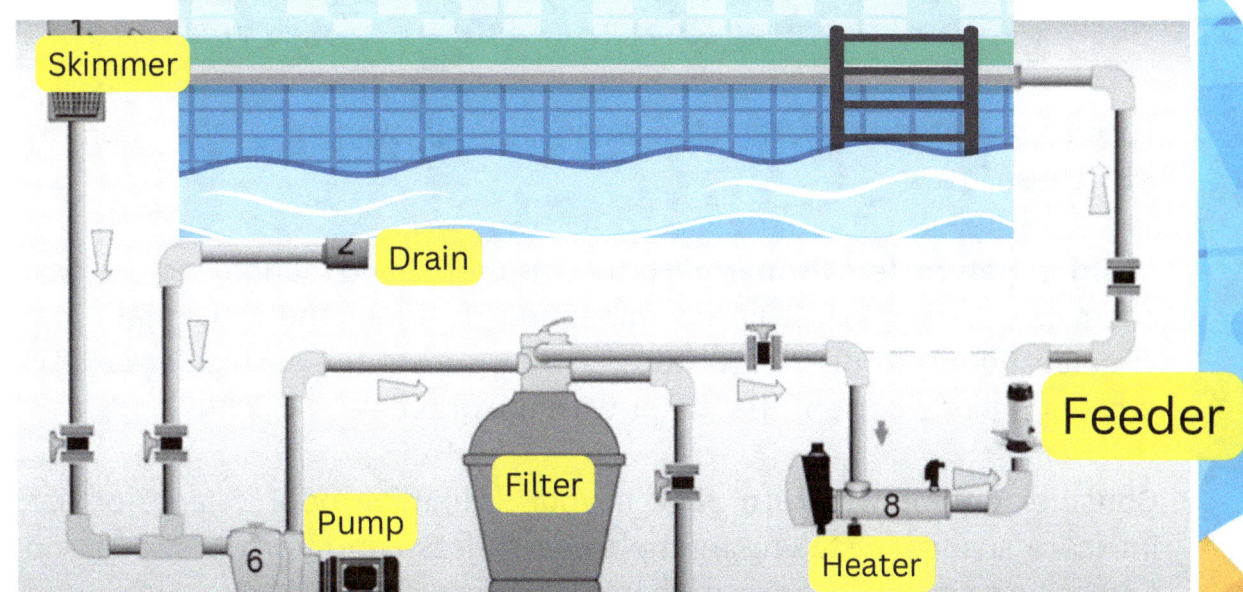

Pool Anatomy

It helps keep the water clean. There are majorly 3 different kinds of filters- sand, cartridge, and DE (diatomaceous earth), each with its own advantages and maintenance needs.

- The pipes carry the water from the pump to the filter and back to the pool through the return jets. These jets help distribute the filtered water back into the swimming pool, promoting circulation and clearness.

Pump

How to optimize water flow and distribution in your pool.

To ensure optimum water circulation in your swimming pool, comply with these ideas:

Position Return Jets Properly: For better particle collection and uniform chemical distribution, it is recommended to direct the return jets in a circular motion to distribute water evenly across the surface area. This creates a gentle current that helps with the process.

Consider optimum Return Jets: If your swimming pool is large or has intricate shapes, installing multiple return jets can improve circulation and ensure no stagnant areas where debris can collect.

Change Skimmer and Key Drain Valves: To optimize dirt collection and prevent air from entering the system, it's important to stabilize the flow between the skimmer and the main drain. Try to inspect and clean the pump basket and impeller to guarantee optimal performance. Likewise, keep track of the motor's operating temperature level and look for any unusual noises which can suggest potential concerns.

Appropriately Size Your Pump: To maintain optimal pool conditions, it's crucial to have a pump that is appropriately sized for your pool's volume and circulation system resistance. In the case of smaller pumps, they may require more flow to operate properly, which is not ideal for larger pools.

Check and Clean Skimmer Baskets: Regularly inspect and clean the skimmer baskets to prevent particles from obstructing the circulation system and affecting water circulation.

Keep Proper Water Level: Keep your swimming pool's water level within the recommended range. If it's too low, the pump may not be able to draw water effectively, which can impact circulation.

Calibrate Return Jets: Make sure that the return jets are positioned to promote good water motion and circulation. Adjust them if required to achieve ideal circulation patterns.

By focusing on circulation and maximizing water circulation, you'll preserve clean and clear swimming pool water, enhancing the general swimming experience.

Section 2 : Exploring Pool Filtration Systems

As we understand the significance of water circulation, let's explore swimming pool filtration systems and their contribution to maintaining crystal-clear water. There are 3 major kinds of filters available: sand, cartridge, and DE, each with its own set of pros and cons.

Sand Filters: Sand filters are among the most commonly used pool filters. They include a bed of specially graded sand that collects debris and pollutants as water travels through. Sand filters are low maintenance and have exceptional filtration ability. The clear water comes out from the second pipe after being filtered.

Sand Filter

Cartridge Filters: Cartridge filters utilize pleated filter cartridges to remove particles. They give a high degree of filtration and require much less attention than sand filters. Cartridges must be regularly cleaned or replaced, depending on the model and usage.

Cartridge Filter

DE (Diatomaceous Earth) Filters: DE filters use grids covered with diatomaceous soil, a fine powder made from fossilized remains of diatoms. DE filters use the highest degree of filtering, efficiently trapping even the tiniest particles. Routine backwashing and including brand-new DE powder are necessary to upkeep steps for DE filters.

DE Filter

It is important to adhere to the maintenance guidelines and recommended schedules provided by your pool's filter manufacturer.

Adequate circulation and filtration are essential to maintaining clean and healthy pool water.

Understanding the function of the pump and circulation system, optimizing water flow, and selecting and maintaining the right filter for your pool will help to keep your swimming pool refreshing.

In the next section, we will delve into the important topic of pool safety, so get ready to expand your knowledge and make a splash!

Recap

- The circulation system in a swimming pool is accountable for constantly moving the water, ensuring it travels through the filtering system to remove debris and impurities. It helps maintain appropriate water balance and stops stagnation.

- The pool pump is the heart of the circulation system. It attracts water from the pool, pushes it through the filtering system, and returns it to the swimming pool.

- The pool water needs to flow at the very least as soon as every 8 to 10 hrs. This turnover rate ensures that all the water in the pool travels through the filtering system, properly removing impurities.

- The three major swimming pool filters are:

- Sand Filters: These filters use a bed of sand to trap debris and dirt particles.
- Cartridge Filters: Cartridge filters have a pleated cartridge that catches contaminants.
- DE (Diatomaceous Earth) Filters: DE filters use a powder made from fossilized diatoms to layer a grid as well as capture little particles.

7. Pool Safety and Essential Guidelines

Section 1: Creating a Safe Pool Environment

Greetings, pool owners! As we delve into Chapter 7, prioritize safety and best practices. Our focus will be on discussing the essential guidelines.

What are the most important tools for pool safety?

Below are the critical pool safety tools:

- **Swimming pool Fencing:** Have a physical barrier around the pool area to prevent unapproved entry, especially for children.

- **Pool Alarms**: Different pool sensors can detect activity, such as surface wave sensors, subsurface movement sensors, border alarms, and gate/door alarm systems.

- **Pool Covers**: Swimming pool covers can be either manual or automatic. They help protect the pool when it's not being used, preventing accidental falls or unauthorized access.

- **Swimming Pool Safety Nets:** To prevent accidental falls into the pool, a barrier net is placed over the surface area of the water.

- **Pool Security Signs:** The swimming pool has visible signs that provide essential safety and security instructions and warnings for swimmers and users.

- **Life Ring or Life Hook**: Life-saving tools are readily available and can be thrown to someone in distress while in the water.

- **Pool Action Handrails**: Sturdy handrails are installed on swimming pool steps or ladders to help swimmers safely get in and out of the pool.

- **Swimming Pool Depth Markers**: It is essential to have clear and visible markings on the pool walls or deck that indicate the water's depth.

- **First Aid Kit**: A pool emergency kit should include bandages, antibacterial products, and CPR instructions.

What are the functionalities of various safety tools?

Ensuring the security of swimmers is the primary aim of pool maintenance. Implementing the following safety measures will assist in protecting swimmers:

Pool Fencing
Enhancing swimming pool safety can be achieved effectively by installing a pool fence. This physical barrier serves as a protective measure against unauthorized access to the pool area.

To ensure maximum safety, the fence should be at least 4 feet high and free from any gaps that children can use to gain access. Additionally, the gate should remain closed and well-maintained to ensure proper functioning.

Fence Types

Pool Alarms:

If you're looking for ways to improve the safety of your swimming pool area, consider installing a pool alarm. These digital devices can detect when someone enters the pool area or goes underwater. There are different types of pool alarms available, including surface wave detection, underwater motion detection, and perimeter alarms.

Surface wave detection systems scan the water's surface for any disturbances and trigger an alarm if any are detected. Underwater motion detection alarms, on the other hand, detect movement in the water. Perimeter alarms alert you if someone crosses the boundary of the pool area. It's important to choose a system that best fits your pool's needs to ensure maximum security.

Pool Alarms

Pool Alarm System	Usage
Surface Wave Sensors	Detects disturbances on the water surface, such as when a person or object falls into the pool. Sends an alert when the water surface is broken.
Perimeter Alarms	Installed around the pool area to create an invisible barrier. If someone crosses the barrier, an alarm is triggered, alerting homeowners of potential unauthorized access to the pool.
Gate/Door Alarms	Placed on gates or doors leading to the pool area. Sounds an alarm when the gate or door is opened, providing an alert when someone enters the pool area.
Wearable Alarms	Worn by children or individuals who may be at risk of accidentally entering the pool. These alarms detect when the device gets wet or submerged and emit a loud sound to alert caregivers.

Pool Covers :

There are various types of pool covers available in the market that cater to different needs.

- **Safety covers** act as a barrier to preventing accidental falls into the pool.
- **Solar covers** help to retain heat and reduce water evaporation.
- **Winter covers** protect the pool during the winter season.
- **Automatic covers** offer convenience and ease of use.
- **Mesh covers** allow water to pass through while keeping debris out. Thermal covers provide insulation to retain heat and reduce energy costs.

Solar Cover

Mesh Cover

Automatic Cover

Section 2: Guidelines for Safe Pool Use

What are the tips for a safe pool season?

- Ensuring that everyone knows how to swim is crucial for their safety. Additionally, new swimmers should always be accompanied by someone familiar with lifesaving skills.

- Never permit a child to swim alone.

- Having lifesaving tools readily available in the swimming pool area, such as a throwing rope with rings, a getting-to pole, and a rescue hook, is vital.

- Keeping potential hazards like bottles and toys away from the swimming pool area is essential to ensure safety. Also, electronic devices should be kept far from the pool and damp surfaces.

- Having a secure fence around your swimming pool with a self-locking entrance is a must to prevent children from climbing over, under, or through it.

- Store swimming pool chemicals in a safe location away from the swimming pool location and unreachable children.

- Regularly check your pool for wear and tear, especially inside, for any holes or damage to the lining. Check steel supports on above-ground pools for corrosion and deterioration.

- Stop individuals who have consumed alcohol from using the swimming pool. I have read somewhere that alcohol consumption significantly contributes to water-related fatalities among teenagers and adults.

- Avoid the pool throughout rainfall and lightning storms.

- Use door alarm systems, locks, and security covers when the pool is not used.

- Never leave toys in the swimming pool when it is not being used. These create a dangerous attraction for young children attempting to get to the object in the swimming pool.

What are the best practices for pool property with kids and pets?

- "It is important to always have a grown-up with you when you are near or in the water, just like when crossing the street." This safety rule should be consistently emphasized, like all other rules in the household.

- "No one is watching when everybody watches"- Assign an adult **Watcher** when a large group of kids swims. Keep shifting the role every 30 minutes, but there should be absolute clarity about who is the watcher now. Keep a tag, if possible, to identify the current person. When a child is distressed in water, they may not make noise or flail their arms. It's important to act quickly to prevent drowning.

- Teach kids water safety, let them learn swim lessons, and keep them away from pool drains, pipes & openings to prevent entrapments.

- Use a personal flotation device instead of toys like water wings or noodles for safe swimming.

- Always have a phone, first aid kit, flotation device, and scissors near your pool for emergencies.

- Look in the pool first if the child is missing in the house.

- It's important to know how to perform CPR on children and adults, and keeping your skills up-to-date through regular practice is crucial.
-
- Install a 5-foot fence and self-closing, self-latching gates for pool safety. Encourage neighbors to do the same. Ensure the fence is secure and prevents the child from passing through the top, bottom, and middle portions.

8. Troubleshooting Common Pool Issues

Section 1: Dealing with Water Imbalance

Let's discuss the most common issues faced by beginner pool owners.

Understanding the causes and effects of imbalanced water chemistry

- Swimming pools can become contaminated by people, pets, and debris from the surrounding area.

- Cloudy water in a swimming pool is a sign of chemical imbalance. It could be due to unbalanced pH levels, high chlorine levels, or poor filtration. Algae growth is another symptom of imbalance. Use pool shock treatment and algaecide to prevent or treat it. Swimmers may experience irritation due to chemical imbalances, so promptly addressing the issue is crucial for safety. Be vigilant and maintain a safe swimming experience.

- Balancing your pool's chemicals is crucial for several reasons. Firstly, unbalanced chemicals can cause skin irritations and eye problems. Secondly, it can cause corrosion to your pool equipment. Thirdly, high chemical levels can damage your filter, leading to expensive replacements. Lastly, a balanced pool looks more inviting to swimmers. Remember to balance pH, alkalinity, calcium hardness, stabilizer, and chlorine for a sparkling pool.

- To ensure that your swimming pool stays clean and safe, it's important to maintain water quality. This can be achieved through proper filtration, chlorination, and monitoring of pH level, total alkalinity (TA), and calcium hardness.

- It's recommended to check the pH and chlorine levels daily, ideally before the first swim of the day, to ensure that the water quality has stayed the same over time. Additionally, it's important to note that people swimming in the pool are a primary source of contamination.

pH levels

- It's essential to maintain the proper pH level in your pool to prevent harm to your pool apparatus and surface materials, as well as skin irritation for swimmers,

- If too acidic, the water can cause equipment corrosion, while excessive alkalinity can lead to scaling and murky water.

- Both high acidity and alkalinity can also decrease the effectiveness of chlorine, disrupting its disinfecting abilities.

- The pH scale ranges from 0 (extreme acidity) to 14 (excessive alkalinity), with 7 being the neutral point.

- For best results, it's recommended to maintain the pH level of your pool between 7.2 and 7.8.

Alkalinity

Water alkalinity refers to its ability to resist pH changes, acting as a buffer that prevents sudden shifts. Proper maintenance of alkalinity is crucial for water balance and effective sanitization.

- The ideal range for alkalinity in a pool is typically between 80 and 120 parts per million (ppm). Here's how you can adjust alkalinity levels:

- **To lower** high alkalinity levels in your pool, you can use an alkalinity reducer like muriatic acid or sodium bisulfate. Follow the manufacturer's instructions and add the product slowly, usually near the pool's return jets while the filtration system is on. Monitor the alkalinity levels periodically to track progress and make further adjustments as needed.

- **To raise** the alkalinity of your pool, use an alkalinity increaser like baking soda if it falls below the recommended range. Follow the product guidelines and add the increaser gradually, spreading it evenly over the pool's surface. Let the water circulate for a few hours, then test the alkalinity again. Repeat the process if necessary until the desired range is reached.

Maintaining the proper alkalinity level in your pool is crucial to prevent water chemistry issues. Test your pool water once or twice a week and make adjustments as needed based on factors like rainfall, bather load, and chemical additions. If you're unsure or experience ongoing problems, seek the advice of a pool expert.

Sanitizer Level

The disinfectant level in pool water is called the "sanitizer level," usually chlorine or bromine. This is essential for removing harmful bacteria, viruses, and other pollutants, ensuring the water is safe and healthy for swimmers.

The recommended range for sanitizer levels in a pool depends on the type of sanitizer used.

For chlorine, the ideal range is typically between 1 and 3 parts per million (ppm), while for bromine, it is usually between 2 and 4 ppm. Here's how to adjust the sanitizer level:

Increasing Sanitizer Levels:

If the sanitizer level in your pool is below the recommended range, you should increase it. The best way to do this is using a chlorine or bromine product specifically designed for pools.

It's important to carefully follow the instructions on the product, as different products have different concentrations and application methods.

Typically, you would add the sanitizer directly to the pool water while the filtration system runs. Allow the water to circulate for several hours before retesting the sanitizer level. If necessary, repeat the process until the desired range is reached.

Dilution: Partially drain and re-fill the swimming pool with fresh water to water down the sanitizer focus.

Neutralizer: Utilize a chemical item mainly made to lower chlorine or bromine levels. Follow the guidelines provided by the manufacturer for proper usage and dosage.

Regularly check sanitizer levels in your pool to prevent harmful bacteria growth. Use a reliable test kit or examination strips at least once a week. Avoid excessive levels to prevent skin and eye irritation. Maintain a balance within the recommended range for clean and safe swimming. Consult a pool expert for personalized support if needed.

Preventing scale buildup and Staining

Scale Build-up & Staining

If you notice a white coating around the water lines of your pool, it could indicate issues with your water chemistry. This buildup is caused by inorganic substances, such as calcium, and can be found on surfaces like plaster, ceramic tile, fiberglass, and stone, commonly used in commercial pool. It's not a pleasant sight, but it's important to address it promptly.

Scale Build -up

Staining

Staining or water discoloration in your pool can appear in shades such as black, yellow, or brownish. This is usually caused by excess pool water minerals that break down into their metallic components.

Below are the best practices to avoid scaling and staining:

- Test your pool water for Total Hardness, pH, and Total Alkalinity before adding chemicals. Keep Total Hardness between 175-275 ppm, pH between 7.2-7.6, and Total Alkalinity between 80-150 ppm for optimal water quality. Use balancers to restore balance if needed.

- A monthly preventative treatment targeting both issues is essential to prevent scale formation and steel stains on your appliances. This will protect your pool equipment and remove any fresh metal stains that may have already occurred.

- Regular pool cleaning is essential to prevent stains and buildup. Use a pumice rock for 5-7 days to brush affected areas. Skim the water, brush walls, vacuum, and empty skimmer baskets to maintain your pool.

- To remove mineral deposits from your pool, use muriatic acid. Wear protective gear, and leave it on only briefly to avoid damage.

- Regularly clean the sides to keep your pool clean and looking good to prevent lime and scale buildup. Adding fresh water a few times a year can also help reduce salt and metal concentrations

Section 2: Managing Algae and Green Water

Algae are plant-like organisms that use sunlight, water, and carbon dioxide to make food. They can grow in swimming pools and should be treated promptly to prevent spreading. Although most pool algae aren't dangerous, harmful bacteria and parasites exist.

Algae types , their causes and how to get rid of them :

Algae Type	Causes	Solutions
Green Algae	Excessive sunlight, high pH levels, poor sanitation	- Maintain proper water chemistry by adjusting pH and sanitizer levels.
	Inadequate circulation and filtration	- Brush affected areas and vacuum the pool regularly to improve circulation.
	Presence of organic debris	- Skim the pool surface and clean out the skimmer basket regularly to remove debris.
	Lack of proper maintenance	- Maintain proper sanitizer levels and regularly shock the pool to kill algae.
		- Ensure proper water balance and consider using algaecides to prevent algae growth.
Yellow/Mustard Algae	Poor sanitation, low chlorine levels	- Maintain adequate sanitizer levels, specifically chlorine, to prevent algae growth.
	Lack of proper maintenance	- Brush affected areas vigorously and vacuum the pool to remove algae and debris.
Black Algae	Introduction of spores, poor water circulation	- Physically scrub the affected areas using a stainless steel algae brush.
	Lack of proper maintenance	- Shock the pool with a chlorine-based shock treatment to kill the algae.
		- Use a specialized algaecide specifically formulated for black algae.
Pink Algae	Low sanitizer levels, high temperatures	- Maintain proper sanitizer levels, specifically chlorine, to prevent algae growth.
	Lack of proper circulation	- Brush affected areas and ensure adequate water circulation and filtration.
Blue-Green Algae	Nutrient-rich water, high temperatures	- Maintain proper water balance and limit nutrient sources in the pool water.

*Note that the table is general information; some cases may require extra steps or consultation with a pool expert.

Managing Algae

- Test and balance pool water before use. Check Free Chlorine levels to prevent green water. Keep levels between 1-4 ppm and use appropriate sanitizers if needed.

- Keep your pool clean by skimming the surface, brushing the walls, and vacuuming thoroughly. Empty the skimmer baskets and focus on areas with little circulation. These steps will keep your pool safe and sparkling clean.

- Shocking is another way of controlling pool water turning green. This process eliminates pollutants that can cause algae growth and enhances water purification.

- To prevent algae growth in your pool, use a targeted algaecide. Brush your pool regularly to remove any remaining dead algae.

- Regularly clean your pool filter to remove organic and mineral buildup. Check your owner's manual for backwashing or chemical cleaning instructions. Run your pump and filter continuously for 24 hours after cleaning.

Green Algae

Mustard Algae

Black Algae

Pink Algae

Algaecide

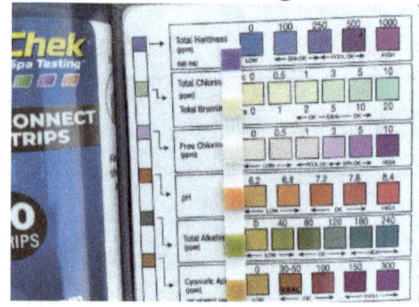

Water Testing

Section 3: Addressing Equipment Problems

Pump

Pool pump issues can quickly ruin the enjoyment of a pool. Fortunately, most problems are caused by a few common factors, making them easy to diagnose and fix. Read on to learn about the most common pool pump problems and how to repair them.

Pump making loud noise: A pool pump is essential for a healthy pool but can make loud noises like grinding or screeching. This might be due to blocked suction lines, a too-powerful pump, or worn bearings. You may need to replace parts or get a less powerful pump for better performance.

Leakage: Check for water leakage in a malfunctioning pool pump. Dripping water may mean a cracked o-ring causing faulty sealing.

Pump basket not filling: If you notice that your pool pump basket is not filling, there's no need to panic, as your pool pump is likely not damaged. You can easily get it functioning properly with a quick fix. To fix the problem, you must prime the pump, which is a complex process. If you need assistance, it's best to seek the help of professionals who are well-versed in this procedure.

Humming Sound: If you hear a humming sound from your swimming pool pump and it won't turn on, it's likely due to a blockage from debris. The impeller may have gradually collected small amounts of debris, leading to a clog.

Pump-sucking air: Over time, swimming pool pump seals can develop leaks, causing the pump to suck in air and prevent proper priming. Clear debris first, then spray shaving cream around the system to find the leak. Replace the faulty part to seal it up.

Filter

The swimming pool filter is a crucial component of your pool that keeps it clean and safe for you and your family to use. Therefore, you must be aware of any issues with your pool filter, whether **sand, DE, or cartridge** filter. If you're experiencing problems, you must solve them immediately for smooth functioning.

No/Low Pressure

There may be an issue if the filter pressure gauge shows zero or close to zero while the pump is running and the valve is in the filter or backwash mode.

Flick the gauge face with your fingernail to ensure the gauge works correctly, and check for any warping that could prevent the dial from moving.

If water isn't flowing through the filter, there may be a blockage before it or a closed/broken valve. Check for clogs in the pump basket, impeller, pipe, or skimmer basket. If the problem is in the air bleeder, turn off the pump, remove the gauge, and clear any debris.

High Pressure

If your pool filter pressure is higher than usual, your filter is likely dirty. Our general recommendation is to backwash your filter (or clean your cartridges) when the pressure is 8-10 PSI above the clean start-up pressure. The supplier's recommendation may differ based on your pool filter type.

A clog or closed valve could cause high pressure in your filter. Check return side valves or heater bypass and make sure they're open. Broken filters or valve parts can also restrict water flow and increase pressure.

High filter pressure is dangerous. Clamshell lids may detach. Normal filter pressure is 8-15 PSI but can range to 30 PSI. If pressure suddenly increases to 40 PSI or higher, turn off the pump and check for internal filter issues or valve problems.

Filter not starting

If your pool filter is not starting, it is usually due to an electrical or motor issue. Let's go through some of the most common causes of this problem and what you should do if you encounter it.

- If your pool filter or pump shuts down due to an overloaded voltage, it could be caused by an overheating filter or pump. To fix this, ensure the fan is not blocked and has enough space to breathe.

- A loose connection can prevent your pool filter from starting. Check all your lines and connections for any broken or torn cables. Replace any loose cords with new ones to restore regular operation.

- A jammed motor can also be why your pool filter is not working. Check your motor for any debris and clean it carefully by hand. Once the motor is free from obstructions, your pool filter should work like new again.

Filter is leaking water around the clamp

If the pressure in a clamshell pool filter gets too high, it can be dangerous. To fix it:

- Turn off the pump and drain the filter tank.

- Remove the clamp band and o-ring, clean and inspect them for damage, then lubricate and reinstall.

- Tighten the clamp band and tap it with a wrench for a better seal. If the container is warped, contact the manufacturer for warranty coverage or replacement parts.

Filter is making a loud noise

Ensure your pool pump is mounted on a steady and level surface to reduce vibrations and prevent loud noises. A whirring or shrilling noise from the filter may be due to bad bearings. Clean the pump basket and impeller to fix a blocked pump and prevent filter overworking.

Heater

The pool heater is not heating the pool

If your pool heater isn't heating your pool, there could be several reasons for it. Some common causes include a dirty or clogged filter, a faulty safety switch or gas valve, a low thermostat setting, a pilot light issue, closed plumbing valves, lack of power source, damaged wiring, poor ventilation, or an outdoor temperature below 60 degrees Fahrenheit.

The pool heater turns off frequently

If your pool heater turns off soon after turning on, try cleaning the filter and checking the safety switches. Adjust the thermostat and reset the timer if needed. Make sure the plumbing valves are open and connected, and replace parts if necessary with the help of a professional.

The pool heater isn't turning ON

Check that your pool heater is plugged in and turned on. If there are electrical issues, reset the breaker or get an electrician to adjust the amperage. Ensure the gas valve is on for startup, and check the pilot light with a mirror. If there's no spark, test the ignition control with a voltmeter. Clean the pilot assembly and remove debris blocking the vents for proper airflow. Check for damaged wiring and contact a licensed expert to handle electrical problems.

The pool heater isn't turning OFF

If you're experiencing an issue where your pool heater won't turn off, it can lead to dangerously high water temperatures and pose a significant risk. It's best to contact a pool service company as soon as possible.

The pool heater emits dark exhaust

In the case of a gas pool heater emitting dark exhaust or appearing black on top, it could be due to excessive heat.

Check the gas pressure on your valve and ensure your heating system has proper air ventilation.

In some instances, poor ventilation can be caused by wind or down-drafting. Installing a high wind stack device on your pool heater can help mitigate this issue.

This is typically a straightforward installation; you can even do it yourself.

Common Equipment Problems

Pool Equipment	Problem	Possible Causes	Solutions
Pool Pump	Pump not turning on or not circulating water	- Tripped circuit breaker	- Check the circuit breaker and reset if necessary
		- Faulty motor	- Inspect the motor for any issues and replace if faulty
		- Clogged impeller	- Clean or unclog the impeller
		- Air leakage	- Ensure there are no air leaks in the pump system and address any leaks promptly
Pool Filter	Inefficient filtration or dirty pool water	- Clogged or dirty filter media	- Clean or replace the filter media as recommended by the manufacturer
		- Inadequate backwashing	- Perform regular backwashing or cleaning cycles according to the filter type
		- Damaged filter parts	- Inspect and replace damaged or worn-out filter parts

Pool Heater	Heater not producing heat or inadequate heating	- Insufficient gas or electricity supply	- Ensure proper gas or electricity supply to the heater
		- Clogged or dirty heat exchanger	- Clean or descale the heat exchanger to remove any buildup
		- Malfunctioning thermostat or control panel	- Check and calibrate the thermostat or control panel
Pool Chlorinator	Inadequate chlorine production or inconsistent chlorine levels	- Clogged or dirty chlorinator cell	- Clean or descale the chlorinator cell according to the manufacturer's instructions
		- Improper water flow	- Ensure proper water flow and adjust as needed
		- Low salt levels (for saltwater chlorinators)	- Maintain the recommended salt levels for saltwater chlorinators
		- Faulty control panel	- Check and calibrate the control panel or replace any faulty components
Pool Timer	Timer not functioning or pool equipment not operating at the desired times	- Incorrect timer settings	- Double-check the timer settings and adjust as needed
		- Faulty timer mechanism	- Inspect the timer mechanism for any malfunctions and replace if necessary
		- Electrical issues	- Verify the electrical connections and address any wiring issues if present

9. Off-Season Maintenance and Winterizing

Section 1: Preparing for the Off-Season

Let's discuss the most off-season maintenance practices.

Why is off-season maintenance important?

Maintaining your pool is a year-round responsibility, even when it's not being used. Neglecting your swimming pool during colder weather can lead to damages that will eventually result in expensive repairs and a shorter lifespan for your pool. Avoiding this mistake to save money, in the long run, is important

Pool Chemicals

Regarding pool maintenance, it's important to take preventative measures to keep the water clean and safe. Before closing your swimming pool for the fall, add algaecide and chlorine to the water in the proper amounts. Avoid overdoing it with chlorine, as it can bleach the pool's lining. Following these steps will help protect the water from harmful bacteria and algae while the pool is not in use.

It's also important to add chemicals to the pool in the early spring before it warms up. This will help the pool clean itself more efficiently, making reopening easier when the time comes. Always follow the chemical instructions carefully to ensure the best results.

Maintaining water level

Maintain correct water levels to avoid system icing up. Lower water levels before fall. Drain pool filter, pump, and heater.

Keep water levels at least 6 inches below the skimmer. Discard unused pool chemicals before they expire. Get new chemicals in early spring for best results.

Winterize by removing debris

To maintain your pool, clean it thoroughly before closing it for the season and cover it with a winterized pool cover. Vacuum the cover before reopening it, and use a skimmer basket to remove floating debris.

Vacuum the bottom and scrub the walls to remove algae and dirt when preparing for summer. This will ensure proper maintenance and a carefree summer in your pool.

Open the Swimming Pool Early

When winter ends, and the temperature rises, microorganisms in the pool become active again and grow rapidly. Treating the water before the weather gets warm is best to ensure it's safe. Clean and treat the pool with chemicals after the last frost for optimal functionality.

Steps to clean and prepare your pool for the colder months

To prepare your swimming pool for the winter season, it's best to start the winterizing process once the season is over and the temperature consistently drops to 65 degrees F or below.

Starting too early may cause algae growth due to warmer temperatures. Allow yourself a week to complete the process, as several steps must be performed over a few days.

- **Take out pool accessories**

To prepare your swimming pool for winter, take out accessories like skimmer baskets, cleansers, ladders, and steps. Remove the solar coverings as well and hose off any dust and algae. Let the items dry thoroughly and store them safely for the winter.

- **Clean the debris**

Keep your pool clean by removing leaves and debris with a skimmer net and pool vacuum.

Brush the floor and sides thoroughly. Cover the pool between cleanings to prevent dirt buildup.

- **Maintain the water chemistry**

Test the water chemistry before closing the pool. Ensure alkalinity is 80-150 ppm, pH is 7.2-7.6, calcium hardness is 175-225 ppm, and chlorine is 1-3 ppm. Adjust levels, but balance alkalinity before pH. Err on the high side as levels decrease over time.

- **Lower the water level**

To prepare your pool for winter in areas with freezing temperatures, it's important to use a skimmer cover. If you don't have one, you'll need to lower the water level by about a foot if you have a mesh cover and half a foot for solid covers before closing it up. Depending on how you remove the water, this process may take a day or two.

- **Drain and also store the devices**

To avoid damage in freezing temperatures, drain pipes, and tools. Clear pool lines with a blower, plug with expansion plugs and add antifreeze. Drain and store filters and pumps indoors.

- **Shock and algaecide**

Add shock and algaecide to your pool before closing to eliminate microorganisms and algae. Follow package instructions and distribute chemicals evenly throughout the pool. For chlorine shock, don't add it at the same time as algaecide.

- **Cover the pool**

When covering your pool, choose between a safety cover for maximum protection or a winter cover for convenience. Make sure it fits tightly and has no holes or tears.

Section 2: Winterizing Your Pool

How to protect your pool from freezing temperatures and winter weather conditions?

Protect your swimming pool tools from freezing temperatures with these helpful suggestions.

To prevent freezing:

- Keep the pool pump running in temperatures below freezing.
- Use a freeze-defense device to turn on the pump at around 34 degrees automatically.
- Check visually when the temperature drops to 34 degrees.
- Keep your swimming pool clean to prevent freezing.
- Check for debris in skimmers and the drain, and clean the skimmer baskets daily.
- Maintain the correct water level to avoid damage to your pump.
- To prevent frozen pipes, remove drainpipe plugs or open the backwash line.

Tips on winterizing your pool

Winterizing your pool is different from just shutting it down. It marks the end of the swimming season and means that the pool will be unused for several months. In this process, the equipment is turned off, devices are removed, and water is drained from the lines and vessels.

- **Remove Ladders**

Loosen the ladder anchor socket bolt, and knock it down with a heavy wrench. Inspect the ladder for cracks, and tighten bolts. Store handrails, fill spouts, eyeball fittings, pool cleaners, and skimmer baskets in a safe place for spring.

- **Balance Water Chemistry**

To winterize your pool, balance the water chemistry by testing and adjusting chemicals a few days before closing. Use these ranges: pH 7.4-7.6 ppm, Total Alkalinity 80-120 ppm, Calcium Hardness 200-400 ppm, and Chlorine 2.0-4.0 ppm. Brush and shock the pool before closing to remove algae and organic materials.

- **Clean the pool**

Before covering the pool for winter, make sure to thoroughly skim, vacuum, and brush it in that order. Leave no debris behind and give it a final skim if needed. The pool should be spotless when covered to ensure it looks great in the spring. Any remaining debris or algae can weaken the winterizing chemicals that protect the collection during the colder months.

- **Lower the Water Level**

Use a skimmer plug to winterize your inground pool. Lower the water level 6-12 inches below the floor tiles for safety covers. For solid surfaces, lower the water a few inches below the skimmer. Don't decrease the water level by more than 18 inches to avoid damaging your safety cover.

- **Turn off System Components**

To winterize your pool heating system: turn off gas and drain copper tubing, open drainpipe connects, turn off power at the circuit breaker, remove timer pets, and disconnect unused electric components.

- **Add Winter Closing Set Chemicals**

For pool closing, use a chlorine-free kit that includes shock, algaecide, and preventers. Refrain from shock before adding algaecide, as it can make it ineffective.

- **Drain Pump and Filter**

To keep your pool in winter, inspect DE and cartridge filters. Hose down DE grids and check for cracks and stains. Clean cartridge filters, lubricate o-rings and replace filter media.

This ensures optimal filter performance when reopening the pool in spring.

- **Burn Out Water Lines**

Prevent freezing damage in your in-ground pool by blowing out the lines with an air compressor or high-volume blower. Use pool plugs and skimmer guards to protect against expanding ice. Adding safe pool antifreeze is also recommended.

- **Cover the Pool**

To winterize your inground pool, skim it once more and wipe down the cover to prevent debris. Check for tears in the cover and move them away from the pump. Apply patches as needed.

Tips for reopening and preparing the pool for the next swimming season

Enjoy the warmer weather and brighter spring days by preparing your pool for the new season. Follow these simple tips to open your pool and dive right in!

Here are some essential tips to help you prepare your swimming pool for the upcoming season:

- **Remove the Winter Cover**: Carefully remove the cover, ensuring it is clean and dry before storing it for future use.

- **Skim and Clean:** Use a pool skimmer to remove any leaves, debris, or insects that may have accumulated on the water's surface. Clean the pool walls and floor with a pool brush and vacuum to remove any remaining dirt.

- **Check Water Level:** Ensure the water level is appropriate by adding or draining water as needed.

- **Test Water Chemistry**: Examine the pool water and adjust the pH, alkalinity, and sanitizer levels to the recommended range. Properly balanced water chemistry is essential for safe and enjoyable swimming.

Shock the Pool: Add a pool shock treatment to eliminate any bacteria and contaminants that may have accumulated during the off-season.

Inspect Equipment: Check all pool equipment, such as pumps, filters, heaters, and skimmers, for any damage or wear. Replace or repair any defective parts.

Clean Filters: Clean or replace pool filters to ensure maximum filtration efficiency.

Check Safety Equipment: Check and test all safety equipment, such as pool alarms and fencing, to ensure they are in good working condition.

Prime the Pump: If the pool pump is winterized, ensure it is properly primed and ready for operation.

Run the System: Turn on the pool pump and filtration system and let it run for several hours to circulate and filter the water thoroughly.

Add Pool Chemicals: After the water has circulated and the pump has run, add the necessary pool chemicals to balance the water chemistry.

Brush and Vacuum: Brush the pool walls and floor again to remove any remaining dirt, and vacuum the pool to remove it.

Set up Pool Accessories: Install pool accessories such as ladders, diving boards, and pool furniture, ensuring they are safe and secure.

Enjoy your Pool: Once everything is set up and the water is crystal clear, your pool is ready for a season of fun and enjoyment!

By following these steps and performing regular maintenance throughout the swimming season, you can keep your pool in excellent condition and provide everyone with a safe and refreshing swimming experience. Happy swimming!

Steps/Workflow - Winterize and Reopening

Winterizing Steps	Reopening Steps
1. Clean the pool thoroughly	1. Remove the winter cover
2. Balance water chemistry	2. Skim and clean the pool
3. Shock the pool	3. Check water level
4. Backwash the filter	4. Test water chemistry
5. Lower water level	5. Shock the pool
6. Remove and store accessories	6. Inspect equipment
7. Drain pool equipment	7. Clean filters
8. Install winter cover	8. Check safety equipment
9. Winterize plumbing lines	9. Run the system
10. Regularly monitor	10. Add pool chemicals
	11. Shock again (optional)
	12. Brush and vacuum the pool
	13. Set up pool accessories
	14. Enjoy your pool!

Winterize

93

10. Glossary & Frequently Asked Questions (FAQs)

Section 1: Glossary

Acid is a chemical that contains hydrogen and can dissolve steel. It reacts with bases to create salts and counteracts alkaline materials.

Acid demand refers to the amount of acid required to lower the pH of swimming pool water to the correct level.

Algae are tiny plants that can be deposited in swimming pools or spa water by wind, rain, and dust.

Algaecide is a natural or artificial substance that kills, destroys, or controls algae.

Alkaline refers to a condition where the pH of water is above 7.0 on the pH scale. It is the opposite of acidic.

An **automatic swimming pool cleaner** is a device that vacuums your pool automatically.

Backwash refers to reversing water flow through the filter to clean the filter elements.

Bacteria are tiny organisms living in pool water, some of which can cause infection or illness.

The **base** is a chemical of an alkaline nature that reacts with acids to form salts and neutralizes acidic materials.

Base demand refers to the base (or pH increaser) needed to reach the proper pH range.

Black algae are dark spots in pools and could be slimy and tough to remove. It thrives in areas with weak water flow and can embed itself into porous surfaces.

Buffer is a chemical that helps prevent changes in pH.

Calcium carbonate is a buildup that forms on the surfaces of swimming pools when the water is too alkaline, the calcium levels are too high, or the overall alkalinity is too high.

Calcium solidity is measured in parts per million (ppm) and refers to the amount of calcium dissolved in the water.

Calcium hypochlorite is a chlorine compound that uses calcium as a carrier salt for application.

A **chelating agent** is a chemical substance that prevents staining and scaling by locking up iron, copper, or calcium. It is also known as a withdrawing agent.

Chlorine is the most commonly used bacteria-killing agent for recreational water treatment. It is available in different forms, including chlorine gas in cylinders, calcium hypochlorite, and chlorinated isocyanurates.

Chlorine demand refers to the chlorine required to establish a stable and recurring amount for proper sanitation.

Chlorine residual is the amount of chlorine available after the chlorine demand has been met or bound up in chloramines.

A **clarifier** is a product that causes fine suspended particles in water to combine into filterable or vacuumable clusters.

Combined chlorine refers to chlorine that is chemically bonded to other substances.

Corrosion is the effect of an acidic environment where pH and/or alkalinity are very low.

Cyanuric acid is a chemical substance added to pool water to reduce chlorine deterioration caused by the sun's ultraviolet rays.

Diatomaceous Earth (DE): DE filters use a powdery filtering system made of diatom skeletal remains, a type of plankton.

Dehumidifiers: Heating a swimming pool can cause excess moisture, leading to mold growth. Use a dehumidifier to prevent this.

Design and build: Comprehensive layout and construction of a swimming pool to a concurred specification, collaborating with a pool specialist.

Drain: The main drain is a plumbing fixture in pools, spas, and hot tubs, located at the bottom.

Electric heaters: Swimming pool water can be heated using electrical resistance heaters or solar heating systems. These types of heaters are best suited for smaller-sized residential pools.

Electrical design: The pool designer created the style and blueprint for the electrical system that operates the pool.

Filtering System: Swimming pools use filtering systems to stay clean. The two popular options are sand and glass filters. Sand filters are cheaper and need sand replaced every 3-5 years, while glass filters are more expensive but can last up to 15 years.

Fittings: Swimming pool installations consist of drain pipes and other pipe components that pump water around your pool.

Filter: Filters are used to remove particles from water. Sand, cartridge, and diatomaceous earth are the most common types in pools and spas.

Flow Rate: The measurement of water that flows past a marked point within a specific time frame, such as the number of gallons that move past a point in one minute, is referred to as gallons per minute or gpm.

Free Chlorine: Steps the quantity of chlorine in a swimming pool undisturbed by impurities; contaminated chlorine is called "consolidated chlorine."

Free-form pool: Free-form pools do not adhere to a particular form but are characterized by their free-flowing curves.

Green Algae: This type of algae can turn water green and murky. It is a free-floating organism that is common and easy to clean up.

Gas heaters: Gas heaters are cheaper to buy and heat pools quickly, regardless of the temperature. However, they require more maintenance.

Hand Skimmer: This display is fixed to a structure and connected to a telescopic pole for removing large floating debris like leaves and insects from the water's surface.

Heating: Maintaining an appropriate temperature in a swimming pool is crucial to ensure its water balance and swimmers' comfort. Pool heating options are diverse and can significantly impact the overall experience of enjoying the pool.

Hardness: The amount of dissolved calcium and magnesium in water is measured in ppm (parts per million).

Infinity Pool: Infinity pools are designed to blend seamlessly with natural surroundings, such as lakes or oceans.

Inground pools: Inground pools are swimming pools that are permanently built into the ground, typically found in backyard areas.

Iron: There is a metal often found in tap water that can cause it to appear greenish, yellow, or rust-colored.

Phosphate: Nutrients that can advertise algae growth if existing in too many quantities in the water.

pH: A dimension of the acidity or alkalinity of pool water, with optimal degrees generally ranging between 7.4 to 7.6.

Sanitizer: A chemical agent, usually chlorine or bromine, kills bacteria and preserves tidy pool water.

Shock: Adding a high chlorine concentration to the pool to rapidly increase its sanitizing degree and eliminate contaminants.

Skimmer: A tool set up in the pool's wall surface that aids in eliminating particles from the water's surface.

Test Kit: A device used to measure and keep track of the pool's water chemistry, consisting of pH, chlorine, and alkalinity degrees.

Total Dissolved Solids (TDS): This refers to the total amount of dissolved substances in the water of a swimming pool.

Vacuum: A tool used to clean the swimming pool floor by gobbling dirt and particles.

Water Circulation: Water movement throughout the swimming pool, ensuring even circulation of chemicals and purification.

Waterline Tile: Tiles mounted around the pool's waterline to stop water discolorations and produce a visual charm.

Winterizing: Preparing the pool for winter months to safeguard it from damage and maintain it in good condition for the next swimming period.

Section 2: FAQs

- **How often should I test my pool water?**

Evaluate your swimming pool water at least once a week to keep track of pH, chlorine, and alkalinity levels.

- **What is the excellent pH range for swimming pool water?**

The excellent pH range for pool water is between 7.4 to 7.6.

- **How to avoid and also deal with algae in my swimming pool?**

Regularly shock the pool and utilize algaecide as a safety net if algae appear; clean and shock the swimming pool while running the filtration system.

- **At what interval should I clean the pool filter?**

Clean the swimming pool filter at least once a month or as needed, based on the filter's kind and swimming pool use.

- **Can I use household bleach to sanitize my pool?**

Use pool-grade chlorine or other sanitizers for a clean pool, not household bleach.

- **What steps should I take to winterize my pool?**

To winterize your pool, balance the water chemistry, lower the water level, clean and store accessories, and add winterizing chemicals.

- **Is it safe to swim immediately after adding pool chemicals?**

It's best to wait until the pool chemicals have dispersed and the water is balanced before swimming, which typically takes 30 minutes to an hour

- **How can I prevent and remove stains in my pool?**

Use a metal sequestrant to prevent metal stains in your pool. Consult a pool expert or use a stain remover if stains are present.

- **What should I do if my pool water is cloudy?**

To enhance the clarity of the pool water, it is advisable to examine and regulate the water chemistry, backwash the filter, and run the pool pump for an extended period.

- **How can I keep leaves and debris out of the pool?**

To keep your pool clean, using a pool cover when it's not in use is recommended. Also, make sure to regularly skim the pool's surface to get rid of any debris.

- **How can I troubleshoot low water flow in my pool?**

Check for clogged skimmer baskets, pump strainer baskets, and pool filters—clean or backwash as necessary.

- **Can I use rainwater to fill my pool?**

Rainwater can refill your pool, but it may affect the water's pH and alkalinity levels, requiring adjustments to the chemical composition.

How often should I backwash my pool filter?

To maintain the proper functioning of the filter, it is recommended to backwash it once the pressure gauge indicates an increase of 7-10 psi from the initial clean pressure.

- **Do I need to drain my pool regularly?**

You usually don't have to drain your pool completely. Instead, performing partial water changes is enough for maintenance.

- **How long should I run my pool pump?**

Typically, running the pump for 8-12 hours daily is adequate. However, it is recommended to adjust the duration according to the pool size, the equipment, and the number of people using it.

- **How can I prevent and treat green water in my swimming pool?**

To prevent green water in your pool, regularly test and balance the pool water's chemistry, use algaecide as a preventive measure, and shock the pool as needed.

- **How often should I clean up the swimming pool skimmer and pump baskets?**

For optimal water circulation and filtration, cleaning the swimming pool skimmer and pump baskets regularly is recommended. Regularly clean the skimmer and pump baskets to guarantee proper water circulation and filtration.

- **How should I take care of the pool ladder and handrails?**

It is important to clean and inspect the pool ladder and handrails regularly for any signs of rust or damage. If any issues are found, they should be replaced as necessary.

- **Can I run the pool pump at night?**

Running the pool pump during off-peak hours can help save on energy costs, but it is important to ensure that the pump runs for at least 6-8 hours each day to maintain proper water circulation and filtration.

11. Pool Maintenance Logbook

Table 1: Pool Water Chemistry Log

Date	Time	pH Level	Chlorine Level (ppm)	Alkalinity Level (ppm)

Table 2: Pool Maintenance Schedule

Task	Frequency	Last Completed	Next Due
Skimming	Daily		
Brushing	Weekly		
Vacuuming	Weekly		
Backwashing	Monthly		
Filter Cleaning	Bi-monthly		
Shock Treatment	As Needed		
Equipment Inspection	Monthly		
Water Chemistry Testing	2-3 times per week		
Chemical Balancing	Weekly or as needed		
Winterization	Seasonal (Fall)		

Table 3: Pool Water Test Results

Date	Free Chlorine (ppm)	Total Chlorine (ppm)	Combined Chlorine (ppm)	pH	Alkalinity (ppm)	Calcium Hardness (ppm)

Table 4: Pool Chemical Inventory

Chemical	Quantity (lbs/gallons)	Date of Purchase	Expiry Date
Chlorine Tablets	lbs		
pH Increaser	lbs		
Algaecide	gallon		
Calcium Hardness	lbs		

Table 5: Pool Equipment Maintenance Log

Equipment	Last Maintenance	Next Maintenance	Notes
Pool Pump			
Pool Filter			
Pool Heater			
Automatic Cleaner			

Table 6: Pool Cleaning Log

Date	Time	Skimming (Yes/No)	Vacuuming (Yes/No)	Brushing (Yes/No)	Backwashing (Yes/No)

Table 7: Pool Maintenance Expenses

Date	Expense Description	Amount ($)	Receipt Attached (Y/N)
	Pool Chemicals		
	Pool Cleaning Service		
	Pool Equipment Repair		
	Pool Vacuum		
	Pool Skimmer Net		
	Pool Filter Cartridge		
	Water Testing Kit		
	Algaecide		
	Pool Brush		
	Pool Cover		

Table 8: Pool Safety Checklist

Date	Gate Latch (Y/N)	Pool Fence (Y/N)	Pool Alarm (Y/N)	First Aid Kit (Y/N)	No Diving Sign (Y/N)	Life Ring (Y/N)	Emergency Contacts

To ensure the safety of your pool area, it is important to take the following precautions:

- Check that the gate latch is working properly to keep the pool secure when not in use.
- Regularly inspect the pool fence for any damages or openings that could compromise safety.
- Installing a pool alarm can alert you if anyone enters the pool area unsupervised.
- Keep a well-stocked first aid kit nearby in case of minor injuries.
- Display a "No Diving" sign to prevent diving accidents in shallow areas.
- Have a life ring or buoy available for emergencies and as a flotation device.
- List emergency contacts with their names and phone numbers for quick access.

Table 9: Pool Water Temperature Log

Date	Time	Water Temperature (°F)

Table 10: Pool Cover Usage Log:

Date	Time Covered (Start)	Time Covered (End)	Reason for Covering	Condition of Cover

Table 11: Preparation Checklist for Winterization

Date	Task	Completed (Yes/No)	Notes
	Skim the pool and remove debris		
	Vacuum the pool		
	Brush the pool walls and steps		
	Backwash the filter		
	Test and balance water chemistry		
	Add winterizing chemicals		
	Lower water level below skimmer		
	Drain pool equipment and plumbing		
	Clean and store pool accessories		
	Cover the pool with winter pool cover		
	Secure pool cover and check for leaks		
	Store pool chemicals in a dry location		

Table 12: Preparation Checklist for Reopening

Date	Task	Completed (Yes/No)	Notes
	Remove winter cover and debris		
	Refill pool with water		
	Reconnect pool equipment and plumbing		
	Clean and lubricate pool pump		
	Test and balance water chemistry		
	Shock the pool to eliminate contaminants		
	Run the filtration system		
	Inspect pool equipment for damage		
	Clean and vacuum pool		
	Brush the pool walls and steps		
	Check pool safety equipment		
	Add necessary pool chemicals		
	Clear pool deck and surrounding area		

Conclusion

Congratulations on finishing the book! You now have the necessary knowledge and skills to keep your pool clean and inviting throughout the year. As you begin your pool maintenance journey, keep these things in mind.

Regular maintenance is key to keeping your pool clean and safe. Test and balance water chemistry, skim the surface, and clean debris regularly.

Brush walls, steps, and floor to prevent algae and dirt buildup. Install safety equipment like pool covers, alarms, and fences. Understand and maintain pumps, filters, and heaters.

Consult experts for complex issues. Join social media groups and local communities to learn and accelerate the process. Have fun and enjoy your pool!

Remember that pool maintenance can be daunting initially, but you'll eventually become an expert with consistent effort and commitment. Go ahead, jump in, and feel proud of how you care for your pool. Enjoy your swim!

Please let us know how we're doing by leaving us a review.

www.ingramcontent.com/pod-product-compliance
Lightning Source LLC
Chambersburg PA
CBHW082210070526
44585CB00020B/2361